DATE DUE

NO 30 '00			

DEMCO 38-296

HANDBOOK OF LITERARY RESEARCH
Second Edition

by
R. H. MILLER

The Scarecrow Press, Inc.
Metuchen, N.J., & London
1995

R

British Library Cataloguing-in-Publication data available

Library of Congress Cataloging-in-Publication Data

Miller, R. H. (Robert Henry). 1938–
    Handbook of literary research / R.H. Miller. — 2nd ed.
      p.   cm.
    Includes bibliographical references and index.
    ISBN 0-8108-2977-0 (alk. paper)
    1. English literature—Research—Methodology. 2. American Literature—Research—Methodology. 3. Reference books—Literature—Bibliography. 4. Literature—Research—Methodology. I. Title.
    PR56.M54   1995
    820′.72—dc20   94-44091

To my students
and
in memoriam
Flore Frédérique Soffree
(1957–1988)

CONTENTS

ACKNOWLEDGMENTS

Much of the credit for this little book must go to Richard D. Altick, Regents Professor Emeritus of Ohio State University, in whose famous graduate course in research I labored through the fall quarter of 1964. I hope some of his magnificent teaching has borne fruit here, and perhaps a little of his critical acumen.

My deepest obligation is to my English 601 classes for hours of toil, for their patience, and most of all for their painfully correct critiques of my work. Whatever is right about this book belongs to them; whatever is wrong is mine alone.

I continue to be indebted to Flore Soffree's efforts in checking and updating portions of the text of the first edition of this work. Flore died in 1988 at the age of thirty-one. We, her professors and friends, miss her very much.

Lastly I extend heartfelt thanks to my colleagues of the Department of English for their help and support. I hope they will like this book and will want to teach from it.

R. H. Miller
Department of English
University of Louisville
Louisville, KY 40292

INTRODUCTION

The purpose of this book is to help you use research time to your best advantage. It should reduce significantly the hours you spend discovering and consulting reference works and allow you to devote a proportionally larger share of your effort to the real business of research: the study of texts and of ideas.

Chapter I introduces you to general reference books that will help you find information quickly.

Chapter II lists selective guides to topics in literature that survey the scholarship on a given subject or author and present selective bibliographies that you can consult rapidly.

Chapters III through VII deal more exhaustively with library research problems that are common to the study of English and American literature and that require fuller use of library research materials. Here is a brief breakdown of these chapters:

The citation numbers do not run consecutively from chapter to chapter. The first digit of each number refers to the chapter number; i.e., Chapter III entries begin with 301, Chapter IV with 401, etc.

- Each chapter is presented in two parts. The first consists of a flowchart indicating the order in which library materials can be consulted for maximum efficiency. The rationale of the flowchart is time-effective; that is, its purpose is to direct you to the item(s) that will provide the largest amount of information first, which in many cases will keep you from searching through resources that duplicate one another. In the charts, items printed on the same level complement one another by providing similar but not completely overlapping coverage, either of a chronological period or of a body of information. Items printed on staggered levels overlap, but the lower item(s) offer less comprehensive coverage than items on higher levels. As you become more familiar with the items, you will find that you can move almost instinctively to the item that best serves your needs without traveling the whole route of the chart.

- The second part of each chapter consists of annotations of the items. For each item a short-title bibliographical citation and a brief critical annotation are provided. (The bibliographical citations presented special problems, since so many of these books have changed publishers over the years, and many more have been brought out in various reprint formats. In each citation I have tried to list only the most recent publishing information.) At the close of each bibliographical citation I have also included the Library of Congress call number. There may be some minor variation in the numbers as they are used in your library. The purpose of the critical annotations is to acquaint you with the scope and nuances of each item as it relates to the research problem being dealt with, and to explain how each serves its function in the process. Rather than duplicate information about each item when it reappears in later chapters, I have included cross-references to earlier annotations. Some items, such as the British Library Catalogue, appear several times, since they serve various functions.

- At the end of the bibliographical entries for each of these chapters I have included a set of sample problems with an analysis of each problem that shows ways in which the references discussed in the chapter might be used. Also included are exercises that test your knowledge of and familiarity with the references.

Chapters VIII and IX discuss guides to manuscripts and collections, and to dissertations, respectively.

As you become more skilled in using reference sources, you will skip over steps in the procedure or move directly to a particular source, because you will have discovered from previous experience that this or that item provides exactly the information you are seeking. This actually is my purpose in suggesting to you a particular method, because for the beginner some procedure is better than none at all, and even though at some later point you may take issue with a procedure I recommend, for the beginner it may still be preferable to a blind search that perhaps leads nowhere. I suppose ultimately that we all manage somehow to stumble onto the information we need and that serendipity plays a larger role in what we do than we would care to admit, but, again, some method is to be preferred over none. You should treat this book as a means to an end, not as an end in itself. The purpose of research is to deepen our understanding, not to accumulate lists. Often we are required to spend too much time searching through library sources, or too often we simply neglect that responsibility and produce poorly informed scholarship. In the future, computer data bases will solve many of our problems. At the moment there are several data bases available that make searching a much pleasanter and more efficient task. As of this writing the MLA Bibliography, 306, can be searched by computer back through 1963, and several major bibliographies are now going on-line, including the British Library Catalogue (316), the various H. W. Wilson indexes, the Wing Short-Title Catalogue (606), among others. Full computerization is still several years off, however, and until it comes this book can provide some guidance as you seek your way among the many valuable but often perplexing basic library resources now available.

Since the plan of this book has always been to include only items that are essential, many useful resources have had to be omitted. Because I believe that most current research guides are too detailed to be helpful, I have cut this list as rigorously as I dare. To supplement it I, however, would like to recommend several helpful guides.

Of particular value are the two most comprehensive publications on reference books:

1 Sheehy, Eugene P., et al., comps. *Guide to Reference Books*. 10th ed. Chicago: American Library Association, 1986. Supplement, ed. Robert Balay, 1992. Z1035.1.S43.

This guide analyzes comprehensively the significant library resource tools of all disciplines, giving in most instances valuable information about the scope and limitations of many items. It is particularly useful to scholars of literature who are doing research in related disciplines and need assistance in familiarizing themselves with bibliographical aids in those fields. A beginning point for all who wish to understand library resources fully. Supplement extends coverage through 1990. A semiannual update appears in each March and September issue of the journal *College and Research Libraries*.

2 Walford, A. J., et al., eds. *Walford's Guide to Reference Material.* 3 vols. 5th ed. London: Library Association, 1989–1991. Z1035.1.W33.

As a complementary guide to Sheehy (1), Walford provides fuller coverage of British reference materials and, for other materials, useful critiques that give information not provided by Sheehy. The current edition of vol. 3, which is devoted to the humanities, covers material available through 1990.

Of additional value are the following books prepared expressly for students of English and American literature:

3 Harner, James L. *Literary Research Guide.* 2nd ed. New York: MLA, 1993. PR83.H37.

Complete, detailed (often too detailed) annotated list of reference materials available for literatures in English, covering items published up to April 1992. Helpful, sound evaluations of each item. Necessity for all students of literature; available in paperback.

4 Marcuse, Michael J. *A Reference Guide for English Studies.* Berkeley: U of California P, 1990. PR56.M37.

Comprehensive, authoritative guide to reference resources published in 1989 or earlier for the study of literature in English and related areas. Comparable to Harner (3) with fuller listings and more comprehensive coverage of non-British and American literature but, given its earlier date of publication, not so current. Includes, within literature sections, helpful entries on individual major authors. As with Harner, annotations are often too detailed to be useful.

5 Baker, Nancy L. *A Research Guide for Undergraduate Students: English and American Literature.* 3rd ed. New York: MLA, 1989. PR56.B34.

This brief booklet provides extremely helpful guidance through the standard library reference items. Though it is aimed at an undergraduate audience, it will be found helpful to most students at all levels of study.

6 Kehler, Dorothea. *Problems in Literary Research: A Guide to Selected Reference Works.* 3rd ed. Metuchen, N.J.: Scarecrow P, 1987. Z6511.K4.
A guide to research materials that is more a textbook than a library aid. Makes careful distinctions as to contents and scope of many items. Contains helpful exercises.

7 Wortman, William. *A Guide to Serial Bibliographies for Modern Literatures.* New York: MLA, 1982. PN695.W6.
An especially valuable and reliable guide to bibliographies published serially throughout the world. Helpful for identifying and understanding the various serial bibliographies now available for modern literatures. Lacks up-to-date information on computer data bases.

8 Altick, Richard D., and John J. Fenstermaker. *The Art of Literary Research.* 4th ed. New York: Norton, 1993. PR56.A68.
An introduction to various aspects of literary study, oriented more toward the historical than the theoretical, with helpful chapters on kinds of research, important libraries, research aids, scholarly writing. Also contains a section of library exercises that will try the skills of any accomplished researcher.

9 Gibaldi, Joseph, ed. *Introduction to Scholarship in Modern Languages and Literatures.* 2nd ed. New York: MLA, 1992. PB35.I57.
A collection of essays introducing areas of scholarly study in languages and literatures, each of which is authored by a distinguished scholar in his or her respective field. Useful for identifying new areas of interest in these fields. Each essay includes a detailed bibliography. Areas covered: textual criticism, linguistics, feminist and gender studies, composition studies, ethnic and "border" studies, and other areas of language and theory studies.

I

A QUICK-REFERENCE BOOKSHELF

These books are recommended because they provide basic information in a compact form: either historical meanings of words, biographical information about writers, brief plot summaries, brief accounts of myths or mythological characters, or historical information.

For the student who plans to continue studies, these books are recommended for purchase. Most are now in print.

Handbooks to Literature

101 Drabble, Margaret. *The Oxford Companion to English Literature.* 5th ed. New York: Oxford UP, 1985. PR19.D73.
A useful encyclopedia of English literature, including descriptions of literary works, brief biographies, indentifications of allusions. Contains also helpful appendixes on the calendar, on the history of copyright. Earlier editions of this work contain more information on earlier periods of English literature and a larger number of entries for allusions; so for the Middle Ages and the Renaissance, for example, you may find an earlier edition more useful.

102 Hart, James D. *The Oxford Companion to American Literature.* 5th ed. New York: Oxford UP, 1983. PS21.H3.
The counterpart of Drabble (101) for American literature, includes similar entries on works, authors, allusions, terms, and the like. Also includes a helpful chronological conspectus of American history.

Dictionaries

103 *Oxford English Dictionary.* Ed. J. A. Simpson and E. S. C.
     Weiner. 2nd ed. 20 vols. New York: Oxford UP, 1989.
     PE1625.N53.
     A slightly expanded and integrated edition of *The Oxford English
     Dictionary,* ed. James A. H. Murray et al., 13 vols. (Oxford:
     Clarendon P, 1933). The largest, most complete dictionary of
     the English language, treating words as they have developed
     historically. Entries provide both etymologies and historical
     meanings. Essential for any understanding of words as they were
     used in earlier periods of English literature. Available also on
     CD-ROM.

104 *Webster's New International Dictionary of the English Language.*
     2nd ed. Springfield, Mass.: Merriam, 1961. PE1625.W3.
     The most generally used reference dictionary for the American
     language, retaining use of historical principles in the presenta-
     tion of words. For a more "current" handling of words, see
     Webster's Third New International Dictionary (Springfield, Mass.:
     Merriam, 1966) and its supplement, *12,000 Words: A Supple-
     ment . . .* (Springfield, Mass.: Merriam, 1986).

Dictionaries of Literary Terms

105 Preminger, Alex, et al., eds. *The New Princeton Encyclopedia of
     Poetry and Poetics.* Princeton: Princeton UP, 1993.
     PN1021.E5.
     A dictionary of terms, forms, and movements, usually informa-
     tive, sometimes prolix and confusing. Discussions are detailed
     and generally authoritative.

106 Holman, C. Hugh, and William Harmon. *A Handbook to
     Literature.* 5th ed. New York: Bobbs-Merrill, 1986.
     PN41.H6.
     A compact dictionary of literary terms, more concise than
     Preminger (105) in its definitions. A handy item, available in
     an inexpensive paperback edition. The fifth edition is much
     improved over previous editions. Frequently updated.

Encyclopedias

107 *The Columbia Encyclopedia.* Ed. Barbara A. Chernow and George
    A. Vallasi. 5th ed. New York: Columbia UP, 1993.
    AG5.C725.
    Concise, informative brief entries on historical events, person-
    ages, and the like. Desk-size and hence of special value for quick
    reference. For more authoritative treatment in encyclopedia
    form consult the older *Encyclopaedia Britannica,* ninth through
    eleventh editions, which are still considered scholarly and
    authoritative. For further information about this important
    encyclopedia, see Sheehy (1) AC3.

Classical Studies

108 Hammond, N. G. L., and H. H. Scullard, eds. *Oxford Classical
    Dictionary.* 2nd ed. Oxford: Clarendon P, 1970. DE5.O9.
    A scholarly, authoritative dictionary of classical studies, includ-
    ing entries on myths, antiquities of all kinds, history, literature,
    with appended bibliographies. Detailed, informative accounts
    of many aspects of classical culture. For those who wish less
    thorough treatment of topics, see *The Oxford Companion to
    Classical Literature,* ed. M. C. Howatson (Oxford: Oxford UP,
    1989).

Style Guides

109 Gibaldi, Joseph, and Walter S. Achtert. *MLA Handbook for
    Writers of Research Papers.* 3rd ed. New York: MLA, 1988.
    PE1478.M57.
    An inexpensive, practical guide to matters of style and format
    for students preparing typescripts. Examples are given in
    typewritten form with clear explanations. For writers submit-
    ting copy to journals and presses, it can be supplemented by
    Achtert and Gibaldi, *The MLA Style Manual* (New York: MLA,
    1985), which deals with format for copy to be submitted for
    publication.

110 *The Chicago Manual of Style.* 14th ed. Chicago: U of Chicago P,
     1993. Z253.C57.
     One of the most authoritative style handbooks, which should
     easily answer most complex questions regarding matters of
     format, organization of parts of papers, documentation, copy-
     editing.

II

READY WAYS TO SCHOLARLY RESOURCES

With the proliferation of literary scholarship and the limited time we have to read it in, we have good reason to look about for shortcuts to doing research. The seminar report, the brief critical paper do not require the depth of research that the thesis, dissertation, article, or book demand.

This chapter surveys briefly the many new guides to research that have come on the market and also introduces some old friends that have come to the aid of students in the past. It does not include research guides to individual authors. Those can be found readily by following the process outlined in Chapters III and IV. It includes surveys of scholarship that evaluate, often annually, the work that has been done in a given field. Such surveys are especially helpful, particularly if we wish to find out trends in fields related to our own or to follow shifting emphases in our own.

The most useful items are the reviews of research published variously by university presses or by the Modern Language Association. Each book consists of essays written by established scholars, and the essays are generally of high quality.

Titles in the Gale Guides to Information Sources vary in quality considerably and must be evaluated individually. Like the MLA reviews of research, this series also consists of books containing bibliographical essays that describe and evaluate. Publication of this series ceased in 1985.

The Oxford histories of English literature provide useful essays appended to the texts of each volume. They discuss work done not only on individual authors but also on background materials, on science, philosophy, religion, and the like. Although the earlier volumes are out of date in several ways, many are still valuable.

Recognizing the close relationship between literary studies and rhetoric and composition studies, I have also included a section on the important basic resources in this rapidly growing field. For coverage of the new fields of ethnic and boundary studies and feminist and gender studies you should consult Harner (3), sections Q3690–4000 and U6580–6630. You should be able to pursue more specific research in particular authors and subjects in these areas by consulting Chapters III, IV, and V below and following the directions contained in them.

In almost all cases, with the continued rapid publication of new studies, these "ready ways" quickly fall out of date, so you should notice carefully the cutoff dates of items and remember that they must be updated. This process can be implemented quite easily by following the procedures in Chapters III through VII below.

The items are arranged here by field, chronologically, then alphabetically by author.

General Surveys

201 *The Year's Work in English Studies* [1919–]. London: John Murray, 1921–. PE58.E6.
     An annual survey, in essay form, evaluating the scholarship in English literature, including (since 1954) coverage of American literature. As is usual, quality varies, but this survey does provide an overview of developing trends in literary scholarship. Usually three or four years behind schedule. Indexed by scholar, and by author and subject treated.

English Literature, Period Surveys

Old and Middle English

202 Beale, Walter H. *Old and Middle English Poetry: A Guide to Information Sources.* Detroit: Gale Research, 1976. Z2014.P7B34.

203 Bennett, J. A. W. *Middle English Literature.* Ed. Douglas Gray. Oxford: Clarendon P, 1986. PR255.B43.
     A historical survey of major topics of English medieval literature with excellent and useful selected bibliographies.

204 Penninger, Frieda Elaine. *English Drama to 1660 (Excluding Shakespeare): A Guide to Information Sources.* Detroit: Gale Research, 1976. Z2014.D7P46.

205 White, D. Jerry. *Early English Drama, Everyman to 1580: A Reference Guide.* Boston: G. K. Hall, 1986. PR641.W44.

206 The Year's Work in Old English Studies [1967–]. Annually in *Old English Newsletter,* 1968–. PE101.O43.
A yearly survey of scholarship on Old English culture, consisting of essays on various areas by scholars.

Renaissance

207 Bush, Douglas. *English Literature in the Earlier Seventeenth Century, 1600–1660.* 2nd ed. New York: Oxford UP, 1969, 461–668. PR431.B8.
Bibliographical essays on both background materials and individual authors, fully evaluated and carefully selected, limited only by being somewhat dated.

208 Harner, James L. *English Renaissance Prose Fiction, 1500–1660: An Annotated Bibliography of Criticism (1800–1976).* Boston: G. K. Hall, 1978. Continued in Harner, *English Renaissance Prose Fiction, 1500–1660: An Annotated Bibliography of Criticism (1976–1983)* (Boston: G. K. Hall, 1985); and Harner, . . . *1984–1990* (Boston: G. K. Hall, 1992). Z2014.F4H37; PR833.H37.

209 Lewis, C. S. *English Literature in the Sixteenth Century Excluding Drama.* New York: Oxford UP, 1954, 594–685. PR411.L4.
Bibliographical essays on various aspects of Renaissance studies on English literature and culture, and on major and minor writers. A classic study, though bibliographies are now dated.

210 "Recent Studies in Elizabethan and Jacobean Drama." Annually in the spring issue of *Studies in English Literature,* 1961–. PR1.S82.

211 "Recent Studies in the English Renaissance." Annually in the winter issue of *Studies in English Literature,* 1961–. PR1.S82. A bibliographical survey of the scholarship for the year, written by a noted scholar, with critical evaluations of works, and an appended bibliography of books and articles received for review.

212 Wilson, F. P. *The English Drama, 1485–1585.* Ed. G. K. Hunter. New York: Oxford UP, 1969, 202–238. PR641.W58.
Hunter provides sound essays on background to the theater and on individual playwrights.

See also 205 above.

1660–1800

213 Beasley, Jerry C. *English Fiction, 1660–1800: A Guide to Information Sources.* Detroit: Gale Research, 1978. Z2014.F5B42.

214 Butt, John. *The Mid-Eighteenth Century.* Ed. G. Carnall. Oxford: Clarendon P, 1979. PR441.B83.
Provides a historical review of the period from 1740 through 1789, intended as a sequel to 215 below. Contains excellent bibliographical material.

215 Dobrée, Bonamy. *English Literature in the Early Eighteenth Century, 1700–1740.* Oxford: Clarendon P, 1959, 586–696. PR445.D6.
Somewhat dated but still valuable essays on background studies, cultural movements, and individual writers.

216 "English Literature, 1660–1800: A Current Bibliography" (see 312).

217 Link, Frederick M. *English Drama, 1660–1800: A Guide to Information Sources.* Detroit: Gale Research, 1976. Z2014.D7L55.

218 Lund, Roger. *Restoration and Early Eighteenth-Century English Literature, 1660–1740.* New York: MLA, 1980. PR43.L86. Somewhat limited but carefully selected list, with annotations, to materials covering this period.

219 Mell, Donald C., Jr. *English Poetry, 1660–1800: A Guide to Information Sources.* Detroit: Gale Research, 1982. PR551.M4.

220 "Recent Studies in the Restoration and Eighteenth Century." Annually in the summer issue of *Studies in English Literature,* 1961–. PR1.S82.

221 Sutherland, James. *English Literature of the Late Seventeenth Century.* New York: Oxford UP, 1969, 442–578. PR437.S9. Bibliographical essays on social and political background, on intellectual and cultural movements, and on many individual writers.

1800–1900

222 Conolly, L. W., and J. P. Wearing. *English Drama and Theatre, 1800–1900: A Guide to Information Sources.* Detroit: Gale Research, 1978. Z2014.D7C72.

223 DeLaura, David J., ed. *Victorian Prose: A Guide to Research.* New York: MLA, 1973. PR785.D4. Bibliographical essays by scholars on the following: general materials, Macauley, the Carlyles, Newman, Mill, Ruskin, Arnold, Pater, the Oxford Movement, Victorian churches, critics, unbelievers.

224 Faverty, Frederic E., ed. *The Victorian Poets: A Guide to Research.* 2nd ed. Cambridge: Harvard UP, 1968. PR593.F3. Bibliographical essays on the following: general materials, Tennyson, R. Browning, E. B. Browning, Fitzgerald, Clough, Arnold, Swinburne, the Pre-Raphaelites, Hopkins, the later Victorian poets.

225 Ford, George H., ed. *Victorian Fiction: A Second Guide to Research.* New York: MLA, 1978. PR871.V5.

Should be considered a complement to Stevenson (234). This guide updates the various chapters of the earlier guide and adds chapters on Butler and R. L. Stevenson.

226 Horsman, Alan. *The Victorial Novel.* Oxford: Clarendon P, 1990. PR871.H67.
Covers the development of the English novel from 1832 to 1880, with excellently chosen bibliographies of authors and issues.

227 Houtchens, Carolyn Washburn, and Lawrence H. Houtchens, eds. *The English Romantic Poets and Essayists: A Review of Research and Criticism.* 2nd ed. New York: MLA, 1966. PR590.H6.
Now somewhat out of date, a sound collection of bibliographical essays on Romantic figures not covered in Jordan (229 below), including Blake, Lamb, Hazlitt, Scott, Southey, Campbell, Moore, Landor, Hunt, DeQuincey, and Carlyle.

228 Jack, Ian. *English Literature, 1815–1832.* Oxford: Clarendon P, 1963. PR457.J24.
Full bibliographical essays on important materials for background studies, cultural happenings, and on individual authors.

229 Jordan, Frank, ed. *The English Romantic Poets: A Review of Research and Criticism.* 4th ed. New York: MLA, 1985. PR590.J6.
A thorough, discriminating series of bibliographical essays on the Romantic period, including a chapter on the movement itself and chapters on Blake, Wordsworth, Coleridge, Byron, Keats, Shelley.

230 McKenna, Brian. *Irish Literature, 1800–1875: A Guide to Information Sources.* Detroit: Gale Research, 1978. Z2037.M235.

231 "Recent Studies in the Nineteenth Century." Annually in the autumn issue of *Studies in English Literature,* 1961–. PR1.S82.

232 Reiman, Donald H. *English Romantic Poetry, 1800–1835: A Guide to Information Sources.* Detroit: Gale Research, 1979. Z2014.P7R46.

233 "The Romantic Movement: A Selective and Critical Bibliography" (see 313).

234 Stevenson, Lionel, ed. *Victorian Fiction: A Guide to Research.* Cambridge: Harvard UP, 1964. PR873.S8.
Bibliographical essays by noted scholars in the field on the following: general materials, Disraeli and Bulwer-Lytton, Dickens, Thackeray, Trollope, the Brontës, E. Gaskell and C. Kingsley, W. Collins and C. Reade, Eliot, Meredith, Hardy, G. Moore and G. Gissing. See also 225.

235 Turner, Paul. *English Literature, 1832–1890, Excluding the Novel.* Oxford: Clarendon P, 1989. PR461.T87.
Survey of literature of the Victorian period, excepting prose fiction, containing useful and current bibliographical materials.

236 "Victorian Bibliography" (see 314).

237 Wilson, Harris W., and Diane Long Hoeveler. *English Prose and Criticism in the Nineteenth Century: A Guide to Information Sources.* Detroit: Gale Research, 1979. Z2014.P795W54.

1900 to Present

238 Altieri, Charles. *Modern Poetry.* Arlington Heights, Ill.: AHM Publishing, 1979. Z7155.A57.

239 "Annual Review Number." Annually in *Journal of Modern Literature,* 1971–. PN2.J6.
Provides essay reviews of scholarship for the year under various subject headings.

240 Brown, Christopher C., and William B. Thesing. *English Prose and Criticism, 1900–1950: A Guide to Information Sources.* Detroit: Gale Research, 1983. Z2014.P795B76.

241 Cassis, A. F. *The Twentieth-Century English Novel.* New York: Garland, 1977. Z2014.F5.C35.
Lists studies of the novel, novelists, and novel theory. Covers scholarship done in U.S. and abroad.

242 "Current Bibliography" (see 315).

243 Finneran, Richard J., ed. *Anglo-Irish Literature: A Review of Research and Criticism.* New York: MLA, 1976. Supplemented by Finneran, *Recent Research on Anglo-Irish Writers: A Supplement to Anglo-Irish Literature: A Review of Research* (New York: MLA, 1983). PR8712.A5.
Bibliographical essays by noted scholars on general works, nineteenth-century writers, Wilde, Moore, Shaw, Yeats, Synge, Joyce, four revival figures (Lady Gregory, A.E., Gogarty, and J. Stephens), O'Casey, modern drama. Supplement contains additional chapters on modern fiction and modern poetry, and extensive supplements to the chapters in the main volume.

244 Gingerich, Martin E. *Contemporary Poetry in America and England, 1950–1975: A Guide to Information Sources.* Detroit: Gale Research, 1983. Z1231.P7G56.

245 Harris, Richard H. *Modern Drama in America and England, 1950–1970: A Guide to Information Sources.* Detroit: Gale Research, 1982. Z1231.D7H36.

246 Mikhail, E. H. *English Drama, 1900–1950: A Guide to Information Sources.* Detroit: Gale Research, 1977. Z2014.D7M553.

247 Rice, Thomas J. *English Fiction, 1900–1950: A Guide to Information Sources.* 2 vols. Detroit: Gale Research, 1983. Z2014.F4R5.

248 Rosa, Alfred F., and Paul Eschholz. *Contemporary Fiction in America and England, 1950–1970: A Guide to Information Sources.* Detroit: Gale Research, 1976. Z1231.F4R57.

American Literature, Period and Genre Surveys

General

249 *American Literary Scholarship: An Annual* [1963–]. Durham, N.C.: Duke UP, 1965–. PS3.A47.

Begun as an annual continuation of Floyd Stovall's *Eight American Authors* (1958), including now additional coverage of recent and contemporary authors. Each section consists of a bibliographical essay evaluating the scholarship for that year. Part I covers Emerson, Thoreau, and Transcendentalism; Hawthorne; Melville; Whitman and Dickinson; Twain; James; Pound and Eliot; Faulkner; Fitzgerald and Hemingway. Part II covers literary topics. Author and subject indexes included.

250 Fenster, Valmai Kirkham. *Guide to American Literature.* Littleton, Colo.: Libraries Unlimited, 1983. PS88.F46.

A guide to the study and research of American literature, divided into two sections: (1) guide to library materials, surveys of literature, studies of critical schools and of intellectual backgrounds; and (2) guide to materials on a hundred selected authors, with strong representation of black writers, women writers, and modern writers.

251 Gohdes, Clarence, and Sanford Marovitz. *Bibliographical Guide to the Study of the Literature of the U.S.A.* 5th ed. Durham, N.C.: Duke UP, 1984. Z1225.L488.

Unannotated but full listing of approximately 1,900 important sources in thirty-five areas of study of the literature and culture of the U.S. Subject and author indexes.

252 Leary, Lewis. *American Literature: A Study and Research Guide.* New York: St. Martin's, 1976. Z1225.L488.

Limited but critically evaluative survey of literary materials, including helpful critiques of scholarship on individual authors.

253 Spiller, Robert E., et al., eds. *Literary History of the United States: Bibliography.* Vol. 2 (see 404).

An enormously valuable set of bibliographical essays on subjects and authors in American literature, covering scholarship to

1973. Provides a discriminating bibliographical introduction to various areas of American culture, as well as helpful essays on the state of scholarship on various American writers.

Beginnings to 1900

254 Kirby, David K. *American Fiction to 1900: A Guide to Information Sources.* Detroit: Gale Research, 1975. Z1231.F4K57.

255 Meserve, Walter. *American Drama to 1900: A Guide to Information Sources.* Detroit: Gale Research, 1980. Z1231.D7M45.

256 Myerson, Joel. *The Transcendentalists: A Review of Research and Criticism.* New York: MLA, 1984. B905.T696.

257 Partridge, Elinore H. *American Prose and Criticism, 1820–1900: A Guide to Information Sources.* Detroit: Gale Research, 1982. Z1231.P8P37.

258 Harbert, Earl N., and Robert A. Rees, eds. *Fifteen American Authors Before 1900: Bibliographical Essays on Research and Criticism.* Rev. ed. Madison: U of Wisconsin P, 1984. PS201.R38.
Bibliographical essays on the following writers: Henry Adams, Bryant, Cooper, S. Crane, Dickinson, Edwards, Franklin, Holmes, Howells, Irving, Longfellow, Lowell, Norris, Taylor, Whittier, and essays on the literature of the Old South, the New South.

259 Woodress, James, ed. *Eight American Authors.* Rev. ed. New York: Norton, 1971. PS201.E4.
A revision of Floyd Stovall's *Eight American Authors* (1958), with bibliographical essays on the following writers: Poe, Emerson, Hawthorne, Thoreau, Melville, Whitman, Twain, James.

260 Yannella, Donald, and John H. Roch. *American Prose to 1820: A Guide to Information Sources.* Detroit: Gale Research, 1979. Z1231.P8Y36.

1900 to Present

261 Brier, Peter A., and Anthony Arthur. *American Prose and Criticism, 1900–1950: A Guide to Information Sources.* Detroit: Gale Research, 1981. PS362.B65.

262 Bryer, Jackson R., ed. *Sixteen Modern American Authors: A Survey of Research and Criticism.* Rev. ed. Durham, N.C.: Duke UP, 1974; and *Sixteen . . . : A Survey . . . Since 1972.* Durham: Duke UP, 1989. PS221.F45.
Bibliographical essays by various hands on modern American authors: Anderson, Cather, H. Crane, Dreiser, Eliot, Faulkner, Fitzgerald, Frost, Hemingway, O'Neill, Pound, Robinson, Steinbeck, Stevens, Williams, Wolfe. Second volume continues coverage through 1985.

263 Woodress, James. *American Fiction, 1900–1950: A Guide to Information Sources.* Detroit: Gale Research, 1974. Z1231. F4W64.

See also 238, 239, 244, 245, 248 above.

Rhetoric and Composition

General

264 Horner, Winifred Bryan, ed. *The Present State of Scholarship in Historical and Contemporary Rhetoric.* Rev. ed. Columbia: U of Missouri P, 1990. PN183.P7.
Six essays on historical eras of rhetorical theory from classical to recent times, each written by an eminent scholar, each including useful bibliographical reviews. See also 271.

265 McClelland, Ben W., and Timothy R. Donovan, eds. *Perspectives on Research and Scholarship in Composition.* New York: MLA, 1985. PE1404.P45.
Collection of thirteen essays on the major areas of composition study, by experts, assessing scholarship done in those areas.

266 Tate, Gary, ed. *Teaching Composition: Twelve Bibliographic Essays.*
     Rev. ed. Fort Worth: Texas Christian UP, 1987.
     PE1404.T39.
     Classic survey of scholarship done on twelve topics, by leading
     experts, in composition research, including essays on such
     topics as literary theory and composition, writing across the
     curriculum, and basic English.

Bibliographies

267 "Annotated Bibliography of Research in the Teaching of
     English" [1966–]. Annually in *Research in the Teaching of
     English,* 1967–.
     Highly selective annotated listing of research on this subject,
     including coverage of dissertations and materials circulated
     through ERIC (see 273). To be used in conjunction with 269.

268 Bizzell, Patricia, and Bruce Herzberg, eds. *The Bedford Bibliog-
     raphy for Teachers of Writing.* 3rd ed. New York: Bedford
     Books, 1991. Z5818.E5B58.
     Extremely useful and compact listing of materials relevant to
     research and teaching in composition; includes informative
     annotations.

269 *CCCC Bibliography of Composition and Rhetoric* [1984–]. Carbon-
     dale: Southern Illinois UP, 1987–. Previously *Longman Bibli-
     ography of Composition and Rhetoric* [1984–1988], ed. Erika
     Lindemann (New York: Longmans, 1986–1988).
     PE1404.L62.
     The most useful annotated bibliography of composition studies,
     limited only by its recency. Coverage of some materials in
     earlier years is provided by R. Larson, in *CCC,* May 1975–1979
     and October 1987–1988. A more systematic retrospective
     bibliography is forthcoming.

270 Hillocks, George, Jr. *Research on Written Composition: New
     Directions for Teaching.* Urbana, Ill.: NCTE, 1986.
     PE1404.H55.

An overview of composition research since 1963, covering seven areas in detail, e.g., composing process, grammar, invention, modes of instruction. Includes extensive bibliography.

271 Horner, Winifred Bryan, ed. *Historical Rhetoric: An Annotated Bibliography of Selected Sources in English*. Boston: G. K. Hall, 1980. Z7004.R5.
Survey of basic texts in and scholarship on five historical periods from classical times to the nineteenth century. Includes helpful annotations.

272 Moran, Michael G., and Ronald F. Lunsford, eds. *Research in Composition and Rhetoric: A Bibliographic Sourcebook*. Westport, Conn.: Greenwood, 1984. PE1404.R385.
Intended as a complementary volume to Tate's earlier edition of 266 (1976), this collection provides sixteen essays appraising research in various areas of composition study, including the psychology of composition, philosophy and rhetoric, grading and evaluation. Helpful appendixes on evaluating handbooks and on writing textbooks. An important and valued source.

273 ERIC [Education Resources Information Center], 1966–.
A data base established to provide access to research both published and unpublished in various areas of education. Includes conference papers and dissertations, as well as published articles and books. Available in hard copy through *CIJE: Current Index to Journals in Education* [1969–] and *Resources in Education* [1967–]. Available on-line from DIALOG; also available on CD-ROM.

III

LOCATING WORKS ABOUT AN ENGLISH AUTHOR OR WORK

The most common task we face is to compile a bibliography of books and articles on a given author or a work or works by that author. This research problem can be divided into two phases.

Phase I allows us to find out if any bibliographies of this author have already been compiled. If they have, then we need only consult them (assuming that they are relatively exhaustive and up to date) and where necessary supplement them with materials collected by following Phase II.

Phase II allows us to compile our own bibliography of books and articles by consulting various retrospective and current bibliographies and if necessary other, more general, indexes. In cases where bibliographies already exist, it allows us to expand them and bring them up to date. Please remember that we are concerned here with lists of works about, not by, an author; that task is handled in Chapters VI and VII.

Please review the flowchart before continuing.

PHASE I:

Purpose: To determine what, if any, bibliographies of a given author exist.

301 Howard-Hill, T. H. *Index to British Literary Bibliography.* 7 vols. London: Oxford UP, 1969–. Vols. 5 (1979) and 7 (1992). Z2011.A1H68.

This extensive bibliography of bibliographies in English literature contains a list of bibliographies published from 1890

LOCATING PUBLISHED WORKS ABOUT AN ENGLISH
AUTHOR OR WORK

Phase I: Locating existing bibliographies
301 Howard-Hill

302 *NCBEL*

303 Besterman & Toomey

304 *Bib Index*

Phase II: Creating bibliographies
A. General bibliographies, English literature
305 *NCBEL*
306 MLA

307 *ABELL*

B. Period bibliographies (see 308–315)
C. General bibliographical resources
C1. Books
316 Brit Lib Cat

317 *CBI*   318 *BNB*   319 *Whitaker's*   320 *Engl Cat*
321 *British BIP*
322 LC Subj Cat   323 Subj Guide *BIP*
324 *Essay & Gen Lit Index* (327 *Biog Index*)
C2. Serials
325 *Poole's* (19th century)

226 *Readers' Guide*   327 *Biog Index*
328 *Brit Hum Index*   329 *Hum Index*
330 *Times Index (London)*   331 *NY Times Index*

through 1979, of English authors. Projected completion of vol.
3 will cover the period before 1890. Our needs here are served
by vols. 5 and 7 of this most valuable but confusing set, which
taken together constitute an alphabetical list by author of
bibliographies (both separately published and otherwise) of
British writers. Both volumes must be consulted in order to
cover any given author fully. See also Sheehy (1) BD494,
Walford (2) 3. 131, and Harner (3) M1355.

302 *The New Cambridge Bibliography of English Literature.* Ed. George
     Watson et al. 5 vols. Cambridge: Cambridge UP, 1969–
     1977. Z2011.N45.
     The most thorough retrospective bibliography of scholarship in
     English literature now published, covering the period from 600
     to 1950, with lists of publications about major and minor
     authors for each period of literary history. Scope of each volume

is as follows: 1, 600–1660, scholarship through 1971; 2, 1660–1800, scholarship through mid-1969; 3, 1800–1900, scholarship through 1967; 4, 1900–1950, scholarship through 1969. Within each author entry in the *NCBEL* a list of published bibliographies of the respective author is printed, items listed in chronological order, including both separately published bibliographies and bibliographies that are parts of books or serials. Generally the bibliographical listings tend to be selective, to list bibliographies of works by an author rather than about that author, and are often limited to separately published items only. To use this reference work first consult the indexes in vol. 5, then the main volumes. For an analysis of the *NCBEL's* subject listings, see 507 below. A new edition is in preparation, focusing on pre-1920 scholarship.

303 Besterman, Theodore. *A World Bibliography of Bibliographies.* 4th ed. 5 vols. Lausanne: Societas Bibliographica, 1965–1966; Alice F. Toomey, *A World Bibliography of Bibliographies, 1964–1974,* 2 vols. (Totowa, N.J.: Rowman and Littlefield, 1977). Z1002.B5685; Z1002.T67.
The best-known subject bibliography in print, Besterman consists of a list, international in scope, of separately published (i.e., under separate cover) bibliographies issued from the beginning of printing through 1963. Besterman lists authors as subjects. It is extended by Toomey, which lists by subject all bibliographies acquired by the Library of Congress from 1964 to 1974, including also authors as subjects. Besterman supplements Howard-Hill by extending coverage back from 1890 to ca. 1500; Toomey supplements Besterman by extending it forward to 1974, limiting itself to Library of Congress holdings. It should be remembered that neither is comprehensive and that both are generally limited to separately published bibliographies and do not include bibliographies that are parts of books or that appear in journals. These are listed from 1937 on in the *Bibliographic Index,* below. Literary materials in Besterman are also available in Besterman, *Literature English and American: A Bibliography of Bibliographies* (Totowa, N.J.: Rowman and Littlefield, 1971), which reprints those sections of the original Besterman having to do with English and American literature.

304 *Bibliographic Index* [1937–]. New York: H. W. Wilson, 1938–.
    Z1002.B595.
    A current serial listing of both separately published bibliographies and bibliographies of fifty items or more that are part of larger works or serials, covering mainly English-language and Continental-language publications. Limited in scope by its relatively recent beginning. This important index supplements and updates all the above items by covering bibliographies published as parts of books and by being relatively up to date. Issued semiannually. An invaluable resource.

At the completion of Phase I you should have discovered either the existence of an author bibliography or the lack of one. If an author bibliography exists, Phase II will allow you to update it. If none exists, it will assist you in compiling one, but only of works about an author.

PHASE II

Purposes: (1) To provide material for a bibliography of an author for whom no bibliographies exist. (2) To supplement and update published bibliographies of an author.

Level A. Bibliographies of English Literature

305 *The New Cambridge Bibliography of English Literature* (see 302).
    As noted above, the *NCBEL* provides coverage of English literature from 600 to 1950, in four main volumes and an index. Under each author's listing you will find a three-part list, first of bibliographies and collections, then of works by, and then of works about, the last arranged chronologically. Cutoff dates for listing scholarship vary from volume to volume, with vol. 1 (600–1660) having the most recent cutoff date of 1971. For a discussion of the *NCBEL* as a subject bibliography, see 507.

306 *MLA International Bibliography* [1921–]. New York: MLA, 1922–. PB1.M44.
    The best-known and most frequently used bibliography of literature, covers English, American, and certain Continental

literatures. Through 1955 it is limited to scholarship done in the U.S. and must be supplemented by *ABELL,* listed below, and other items. Contents are arranged generally by literature (American, English, French, etc.) and within those sections by literary period. Each volume contains an index of scholars. Beginning with the 1981 issue, each bibliography contains a thorough subject index. Can be searched by computer from 1963 on (as of 1994) through the DIALOG system and some other systems, which allows for more up-to-date searching. Available on CD-ROM from 1981 on. Eventually the entire bibliography will be available on-line. Issued annually, usually one year's delay.

307 Modern Humanities Research Association. *Annual Bibliography of English Language and Literature* [1920–]. Leeds: W. S. Maney and Sons, 1921–. Z2011.M69.
A current bibliography similar to the MLA Bibliography but covering only English and American literature and emphasizing British publications, thus providing a supplement to the MLA Bibliography from 1921 to 1955, when the latter included only scholarship printed in the U.S. *ABELL* continues to give wider coverage to British scholarship. It can also be considered an extension of the *NCBEL* (302), since its listings are based on the *NCBEL* listings. Issued annually, though publication tends to lag behind the MLA Bibliography. Indexed by author and subject and by scholar.

Level B. Period Bibliographies

Several of the literary periods are covered by bibliographies which are more selective than the three noted above, but which provide extensive comments on articles and books, and can be valuable to students who are looking for careful selection and evaluation of items. They often list items not noted in the three major bibliographies and hence complement them.

Old English

308 Greenfield, Stanley B., and Fred C. Robinson, eds. *A Bibliography of Publications on Old English Literature to the End of 1972.* Toronto and Buffalo: U of Toronto P, 1980. Z2012.G83.

A retrospective bibliography of scholarship on Old English literature done through 1972, with a few items from 1973. Contents divided into three major sections: general works (including sections on manuscripts, collections, textual criticism); poetry; and prose, with literary works appropriately listed under each category together with listings of scholarship. Emphasis is on literature, so very little of Anglo-Saxon culture is covered here. Index of authors and reviewers, limited index to subjects. See also 206 above.

309 "Old English Bibliography" [1969–]. Annually in *Old English Newsletter,* 1970–. PE101.O44.
A list of Old English scholarship, international in scope, focusing on literary studies, including works in Latin. Areas covered: general, language, literature, Anglo-Latin and ecclesiastical works, manuscripts and illuminations, history and culture, names, archaeology and numismatics, reviews.

Middle English

310 Severs, J. Burke, Albert S. Hartung, et al., eds. *A Manual of the Writings in Middle English, 1050–1500.* New Haven: Connecticut Academy of Arts and Sciences, 1967–. Vols. 1–. PR255.M3.
A handbook to Middle English literature, now in eight volumes. Each volume consists of two parts: one describing and listing the works of a particular genre, the other constituting a bibliography of scholarship on that genre. Contents of the volumes and cutoff dates for the bibliography in each volume vary. At the present time it provides useful bibliographies on such subjects as the romance, carols, the Pearl Poet, Wyclif and his followers, translations and paraphrases of the Bible, saints' legends, instructions for religious, Hoccleve, ballads, Lydgate, among others. Each volume indexed by author and title, and by limited subject.

Renaissance

311 "Literature of the Renaissance." Annually in *Studies in Philology,* 1917–1969. P25.S8.

Now discontinued, this serial bibliography covers the Renaissance as an English (and from 1938 on as a Continental) phenomenon, including important sections on major English writers and Continental authors also (see sections on Luther, Erasmus, Petrarch, e.g.). Index of proper names.

Eighteenth Century

312 "The Eighteenth Century: A Current Bibliography." Annually in *Philological Quarterly*, 1926–1974. Published separately as *The Eighteenth Century: A Current Bibliography*, ed. Robert R. Allen (New York: AMS P, 1979–); cumulated in Louis Landa et al., *English Literature, 1660–1800: A Bibliography of Modern Studies Compiled for Philological Quarterly*, 6 vols. (Princeton: Princeton UP, 1950–1972). Z2011.E6 (Landa); P1.P55 (*PQ*); Z5579.6.E36 (Allen).

An excellent selective bibliography of eighteenth-century studies, with lengthy annotations of books and important articles. The Landa cumulation should be used through 1970, then you must consult the annual issues of *Philological Quarterly* through 1974, and then the annual volumes published by AMS Press. Confusing but well worth the effort. Index, mainly of proper names, in vols. 2, 4, 6 of the cumulation, and to the separately published annual volumes since 1974.

Romantic Period

313 "The Romantic Movement: A Selective and Critical Bibliography." Annually in *ELH*, 1937–1949; *Philological Quarterly*, 1950–1964; and *English Language Notes*, 1965–1978. Subsequently published separately, *The Romantic Movement: A Selected and Critical Bibliography* [1979–], ed. David V. Erdman (New York: Garland P, 1980–). Cumulated in *The Romantic Movement Bibliography, 1936–1970*, ed. A. C. Elkins, Jr., and L. J. Forstner, 7 vols. (Ann Arbor: Pierian P, 1973). PE1.E53 (*ELN*); Z6514.R6R45 (Elkins); Z6514.R6R64 or PN603.R6 (Erdman).

A selective but well-annotated bibliography of scholarship for the literature of this period both English and Continental. The entire bibliography should be searched in the following manner: for 1937–1970 consult the Elkins and Forstner cumulation; for 1971–1978 consult the September isssues of *English Language Notes*; for 1979 and later, consult the annual volumes published by the Garland Press. Vol. 7 of the cumulation constitutes an index to the entire bibliography through 1970. A more sophisticated subject-title index is being planned. The separately published annual volumes (1979–) are indexed.

Victorian Period

314 "Victorian Bibliography." Annually in *Modern Philology*, 1933–1957; *Victorian Studies*, 1958–. Cumulated in *Bibliographies of Studies in Victorian Literature for the Thirteen Years 1932–1944*, ed. William D. Templeman (Urbana: U of Illinois P, 1945); *Bibliographies . . . 1945–1954*, ed. Austin Wright (Urbana: U of Illinois P, 1956); *Bibliographies . . . 1955–1964*, ed. Robert C. Slack (Urbana: U of Illinois P, 1967); *Bibliographies . . . 1965–1974*, ed. Ronald E. Freeman (New York: AMS P, 1981); *Bibliographies . . . 1975–1984*, ed. Richard C. Tobias (New York: AMS P, 1991). Z2013.B57 (Templeman); Z2013.B58 (Wright); Z2013.B59 (Slack); Z2013.B60 (Freeman); Z2013.B593 (Tobias); PR461.V5 (VS).

A selective annotated bibliography of scholarship in Victorian literature, with some brief coverage of nonliterary topics. Procedure for using is to consult the Templeman, Wright, Slack, and Freeman cumulations through 1974, and then consult the annual bibliographies in the summer issues of *Victorian Studies* from 1975 on. All cumulations are indexed.

Modern Literature

315 "Current Bibliography." Quarterly in *Twentieth Century Literature*, 1955–. Cumulated and expanded in *Articles on Twentieth Century Literature, 1954–1970*, ed. David E. Pownall, 7 vols. (New York: Kraus-Thomason, 1973–1980). Z6519.P66 (Pownall); PN2.T8 (*TCL*).

A highly selective but nevertheless useful annotated listing of articles on twentieth-century authors, primarily English and American, but including Continental authors also. Listings are drawn mainly from English-language publications, but some foreign periodicals are included. Pownall's cumulation is to be consulted through 1970, then the separate issues of *Twentieth Century Literature*. No index available at this time.

Level C1. Books

All other sources being found inadequate or in need of updating, you can turn to the more general library reference sources noted below, which index authors as subjects.

316 British Library. *The British Library General Catalogue of Printed Books to 1975.* 360 vols. London: Bingley, Saur, 1979–1987. (For supplements, see 607.) Z921.B87.

This greatest of all library catalogues for the humanities, of the most important collection in the world for English literature, lists not only works by authors but, in the main set only, also lists works about them and so constitutes a critical bibliography of authors of many nations; and since the collection of the British Library is so large, for many authors it contains within its pages the single most exhaustive author bibliography available. This is particularly true for minor authors. Each author entry first lists works by the author, then works about. A massive and often confusing set, but invaluable, especially for coverage of minor authors.

317 *Cumulative Book Index* [1898–]. New York: H. W. Wilson, 1900–. Z1219.C87.

The most exhaustive current index for American and many other English-language titles now issued, this set indexes by author, title, and subject in one alphabet, with authors treated as subjects. Before 1928 its scope is limited considerably, and it contains no listings before 1898. Highly reliable. Available from Wilsonline (H. W. Wilson Co.) as *CBI,* a computer data base.

318 *The British National Bibliography.* London: British Library, 1950–. Z2001.B75.

This item can be thought of as an extension of the British Library Catalogue (316). It is the most reliable current national bibliography of books published in the British Isles received at the British Library under copyright legislation. Its major limitation is its chronological scope, since it first began to appear only as recently as 1950. Each annual cumulation is divided into a subject catalogue (arranged by Dewey decimal system) and two indexes, an author-title index, in the latter of which authors are treated as subjects, with appropriate cross-references to the subject catalogue. Issued weekly, cumulated every four months and annually. Available on CD-ROM.

319 *Whitaker's Cumulative Book List* [1924–]. London: Whitaker, 1924–. Z2005.W57.
A one-alphabet listing, from 1924 on, by author-title–keyword subject, of books listed in the weekly trade publication *The Bookseller* and now in *Whitaker's Books of the Month to Come and Books Abroad.* Authors are treated as subjects. Issued quarterly, annually and in five-year cumulations.

320 *The English Catalogue of Books* [1801–1965]. London: Publisher's Circular, 1864–1966. Z2001.E52.
The most complete available trade bibliography for books published in England, particularly for books published in the nineteenth century. Lists books by author with title and limited subject entries. Arrangement of indexing varies. Through 1961 authors are treated as subjects; thereafter works on authors are found in the keyword-title index (if author's name appears in title). Since it is based on trade publications, not on examination of actual copies of books, its degree of reliability is not so high as that of the British Library Catalogue (316) or the *BNB* (318).

321 *British Books in Print* [1874–]. London: Whitaker, 1874–. Z2001.B72.
A single alphabetical catalogue by author, title, and keyword subject of books available for sale by publishers in the U.K. Published annually. With some skill, this item can be used to locate works about an author when the author's name appears in the title of a given work. Based on publishers' information and hence of limited reliability. Issued monthly on CD-ROM and microfiche. Formerly *Whitaker's Books in Print.*

322 *Library of Congress Catalogs: Subject Catalog* [1950–]. Washing-
     ton, D.C.: Library of Congress, 1950–. Z881.A1U375.
     This extensive set catalogues by subject (with authors treated as
     subjects) primarily books received by the Library of Congress,
     1945–, with some exceptions. Since 1972 the scope has been
     expanded to include all books catalogued or recatalogued,
     including those with imprints before 1945. An important
     source, limited somewhat by its time span. See also Sheehy (1)
     AA130. Issued in quinquennial cumulations, continued by
     quarterly and annual supplements. From 1983 on cumulations
     are available only on microfiche as part of the *National Union
     Catalog,* which can be searched through the *National Union
     Catalog: Books: Subject Index* (excludes entries for children's
     literature).

323 *Books in Print* [Subjects]. New York: Bowker, 1948–.
     Z1215.P973.
     A subject index to *Books in Print,* based on the Library of
     Congress subject cataloguing system, listing books offered for
     sale by firms contributing to the annual listing, *Publishers' Trade
     List Annual.* Treats authors as subjects. Limited mainly by its
     time coverage. While not always reliable, the Subject Guide
     does provide listings of books about authors and may serve as a
     complement to the Library of Congress Subject Catalog (322)
     after 1956. Published annually.

324 *Essay and General Literature Index.* New York: H. W. Wilson,
     1934–. Supplements, 1934–. AI3.E752.
     A cumulative index by author-subject–limited title with authors
     treated as subjects, to essays and articles appearing in anthologies,
     collections, miscellaneous volumes. Useful for locating material in
     these sources through 1947. From 1947 on, consult the *Biography
     Index* (327). This index is often overlooked, but it is essential since
     it indexes parts of books of a miscellaneous collective nature,
     which, since they do not qualify as serials, are not indexed
     anywhere else. Main set covers 1900–1933, supplements 1934–.
     Issued semiannually, cumulated annually.

See also 327 below.

Level C2. Serials

325 *Poole's Index to Periodical Literature* [1802–1881]. Rev. ed. New
        York: Peter Smith, 1938. Supplements, January 1882–
        January 1907, 5 vols. AI3.P7.
        The major index to close to five hundred nineteenth- and early
        twentieth-century British and American periodicals. All items
        indexed by subject, with authors treated as subjects. To be used
        to locate articles about authors living before 1900. Somewhat
        confusing to use. Consult also Marion V. Bell and Jean C.
        Bacon, *Poole's Index: Date and Volume Key* (Chicago: ACRL
        Monograph no. 19, 1957); or Vinton, A. Dearing, *Transfer
        Vectors for Poole's Index to Periodical Literature,* 1 (Los Angeles:
        Pison P, 1967), for correlation of magazine issues with the
        volumes in which they appear; and more importantly for our
        purposes, C. Edward Wall, *Cumulative Author Index for Poole's
        Index to Periodical Literature, 1802–1906* (Ann Arbor: Pierian P,
        1971), which indexes all mentions of authors' names in *Poole's
        Index* and somewhat expands the coverage by locating authors'
        names mentioned in Poole's where they are not listed as main
        entries by subject. See also *Nineteenth Century Readers' Guide to
        Periodical Literature, 1890–1899* (719), as a supplement. To
        locate holdings of periodicals, see 628–633.

326 *Readers' Guide to Periodical Literature* [1900–]. New York: H. W.
        Wilson, 1905–. AI3.R48.
        The most complete modern index to periodicals of a broad
        general nature published in the U.S., of use for locating material
        about an author. Indexed by author, subject, and limited title,
        with authors treated as subjects. Important in that it supple-
        ments the scholarly indexes by covering serials not covered there
        or by the *Humanities Index,* noted below. Book reviews listed
        under author of book's name through 1904, generally omitted
        1905–1975, then included at the end of each annual cumula-
        tion, 1976-. Issued twice monthly September-June, monthly in
        July and August, cumulated at various intervals, then annually.
        Available on computer data base from 1959 on as the *Magazine
        Index,* through DIALOG, and from Wilsonline as *RDG,* from
        1983 on.

327 *Biography Index* [1946–]. New York: H. W. Wilson, 1947–. Z5301.B5.

Indexes materials on individuals that appear in over 1,500 magazines, some books and professional journals, and some obituaries from the *New York Times*. Continues indexing of anthologies and miscellaneous volumes that is covered from 1900 to 1947 in the *Essay and General Literature Index*, (324). Includes a proper name index and an index by profession, in which authors are further indexed by nationality. Issued trimonthly, cumulated annually and triennially. A major resource for locating material published in the U.S. about British authors. Available from Wilsonline as computer data base *BIO*, from August 1984 on.

328 *British Humanities Index* [1962–]. London: Library Association, 1963–. AI3.B7.

A continuation of the *Subject Index to Periodicals* [1915–1961] (London: Library Association, 1919–1962), indexes by subject and by author close to four hundred British periodicals, many of which are not analyzed by various American indexes. Authors are treated as subjects in the subject index.

329 *Humanities Index* (also *Readers' Guide to Periodical Literature Supplement; International Index to Periodicals; Social Sciences and Humanities Index*) [1907/1915–]. New York: H. W. Wilson, 1916–. AI3.R49.

A detailed index to serials of a scholarly or intellectual nature, provides a necessary complement to the scholarly bibliographies (e.g., MLA, *NCBEL, ABELL*) and to the *Readers' Guide*. Indexes in one alphabet by author and subject, with authors treated as subjects. Includes an index to book reviews at the end of each volume. See also its companion, the *Social Sciences Index*, which covers journals in that field. Available as computer data base *HUM* from Wilsonline, from February 1984 on.

330 *The Times Index* [London, 1785, 1906–]. Reading: Newspaper Archive Development, 1907–. *Palmer's Index to the Times (London)* [1790–1914] (London, 1790–1914; rpt., Vaduz: Kraus, 1965). AI21.T44; AI21.T45.

While not so thorough or so informative as *The New York Times Index, The Times Index* provides useful indexing of the great British newspaper, treating persons as subjects. Since the *Times* has been for many years the significant British newspaper of record, it contains information on many British writers. *The Times Index* consists of three units, 1785 (to continue through 1790 when complete), *Palmer's Index* from 1790 to 1914, and *The Times Index* from 1904 on. For coverage of the *Times Literary Supplement*, see *The Times Literary Supplement Index, 1902–1939*, 2 vols. (Reading: Newspaper Archives Development, 1978); and *The Times Literary Supplement Index, 1940–1980*, 3 vols. (Woodbridge, Conn.: Research Publications, 1982), which covers *TLS* from its beginning through 1980. *TLS,* 1940–, is indexed in the *Times Index* and in other indexes, including the *Humanities Index.* For the location of obituaries appearing in the *Times,* see also *Obituaries from the Times 1951–1970,* 3 vols. (Reading: Newspaper Archives Development, 1975–1979).

331 *The New York Times Index* [1913–]. Prior series [1851–1912].
New York: Bowker, 1967–1968; New York: New York Times, 1976–. AI21.N44; AI21.N452.

A subject index to one of the most important newspapers of this century and hence an index to virtually every person who figured significantly in the life of the nation and on the international scene. The *New York Times Index* itself contains not only citations of articles in the newspaper but also brief resumes of those articles. Of particular help in locating materials on persons is Byron A. Falk, Jr., and Valerie R. Falk, *Personal Name Index to the New York Times Index, 1851–1974,* 22 vols. (Verdi, Nev.: Roxbury Data Interface, 1976–1983), and its supplement for 1975–1979, 3 vols. (Verdi, Nev.: Roxbury Data Interface, 1990–), which constitute an alphabetical index to the *New York Times Index,* not to issues of the paper itself. For the location of obituaries appearing in the *New York Times,* see also *The New York Times Obituaries Index, 1858–1968* (New York: New York Times, 1970); and the second volume, *1969–1978* (New York: New York Times, 1980). In *The New York Times Index* obituaries are listed under the heading "Deaths."

Further Biographical Aids

Those familiar with biographical research know that there are numerous reference aids—in fact, too many to analyze in a guide of this size. Further guidance can be found in Harner (3) J540-J600, in Sheehy (1) sects. AJ, AK, and in the various Literature sections under Biographies of Authors, to be augmented by coverage of those sections in the Supplement to Sheehy, and in Walford (2) 2. 548–603. Of particular value is the great biographical dictionary of English figures:

332 *The Dictionary of National Biography.* Ed. Sir Leslie Stephen and Sir Sidney Lee. 63 vols. London: Smith, Elder, 1885–1900; 21 vols., rpt., London: Oxford UP, 1917; 22 vols., rpt., London Oxford UP, 1967–1968. Supplements through 1985. See also *The Concise Dictionary from the Beginnings to 1930* (London: Oxford UP, n.d.); and *The Dictionary of National Biography: The Concise Dictionary,* Part II, *1901–1970* (Oxford: Oxford UP, 1982). DA28.D47; DA28.D56.
This great dictionary of British biography is especially helpful in locating information about little-known authors and in providing concise biographical data on important authors. The *Concise DNB* acts as an index and epitome to the full set. A fuller analysis of the peculiarities and complexities of the set are given in Sheehy (1) AJ217–219 and Walford (2) 2. 5232.

SAMPLE PROBLEMS

1. Are there any bibliographies of John Donne that were published before 1900? How can I locate them?

The question calls for location of bibliographies, further for those published before 1900, so the most likely locations would be Howard-Hill (301) (but only from 1890–), then the *NCBEL* (302) or Besterman (303) under the listing for Donne.

2. I need to locate an article about Elizabeth Barrett Browning that appeared in a popular American magazine published in 1861. How can I locate it?

This calls for the location of an article in a nineteenth-century American periodical, so *Poole's Index,* (325) would be the most likely source. One might also consult the *NCBEL* (302, 305) vol. 3.

3. Graham Greene was involved in some dispute with the State Department in 1952. Where can I find contemporaneous accounts of the episode?

This calls for the location of information about an event having to do with the U.S. government in the 1950s, so *The New York Times Index* (331) would likely provide it. One might also consult the *The Times Index* (London) (330), perhaps also the *Readers' Guide* (326) for magazine coverage.

4. I have decided to do a paper investigating conditions in Ireland during the 1900s, the time in which Joyce's *Ulysses* is set. I have had no experience doing any research in Irish history. Where might I go to gain a knowledge of library resources in the field?

When we need to gain expertise in a related discipline it is always advisable to consult both Sheehy (1) and Walford (2) before we attempt to comb the card catalogues. In both volumes one may find helpful sections on bibliographies of Irish history, in the history sections of each.

5. I need to put together a brief list of magazine articles and anthologized essays on John Fowles, published in the U.S., 1970–1980. Where can I find most of what I need?

Remember that we are trying to find articles about, not by, Fowles. The quickest source is *Biography Index* (327), which analyzes books, magazines, and anthologies and collections, 1947–. One would find partial information also in the *Readers' Guide* (326), the *Essay and General Literature Index* (324), and the *Humanities Index* (329).

6. Have any bibliographies of John Fowles been published within the past three years?

The question calls for us to locate bibliographies of, not works about, so we must turn to Phase I of our search system. The best and most recent information can be found in the *Bibliographic Index* (304), which is the most up-to-date listing of both separately published bibliographies and of bibliographies that are parts of other works.

7. I heard of a book published in the U.S. in 1983 on Doris Lessing. I would like to find its title and purchase a copy. How can I find the information I need?

Such recent information, particularly about the availability of a book in the commercial market, can be found in *Books in Print* [Subjects] (323).

8. I need a quick chronological review of the scholarship done on Thomas Gray, the eighteenth-century British poet, through 1969. Where can I find it?

Such a review over a long period of time can be done most efficiently in the *NCBEL* (302, 305), since under each author section works about an author are arranged in chronological order. While it might not represent a complete listing, it will be a fairly full one.

EXERCISES

1. What books about Jane Austen are still in print in the U.S.? In England?

2. Compile a list of separately published bibliographies of William Shakespeare.

3. Outline a plan for compiling a complete bibliography of criticism of any one of these works: *Paradise Lost, Middlemarch, Titus Andronicus, The Rivals, To the Lighthouse*.

4. Compile a checklist of writings about any British author for whom no bibliography is listed in items 301–304.

IV

LOCATING WORKS ABOUT AN AMERICAN AUTHOR OR WORK

Conducting research on authors and works in American literature is slightly different from that of English literature in that many of the resources differ; however, the basic process is similar.

Start by reviewing the flowchart below, then go to Phase I.

PHASE I

Purpose: To determine what, if any, bibliographies of a given author already exist.

401 Nilon, Charles H. *Bibliography of Bibliographies in American Literature.* New York: R. R. Bowker, 1970. Supplemented by Patricia Pate Havlice, *Index to American Author Bibliographies* (Metuchen, N.J.: Scarecrow P, 1971). Z1225.A1N5 (Nilon); Z1225.H37 (Havlice).

A thorough list, through 1969, of author bibliographies that are either separately published or are parts of books or serials. Entries are not always authoritative or complete, and there are some omissions. Havlice lists only bibliographies published in serials, 1877–1970, and the list is not exhaustive, but it does provide listings not in Nilon. Should always be supplemented by 402 and 403.

402 Toomey, Alice. *A World Bibliography of Bibliographies, 1964–1974* (see 303).

Toomey provides supplemental listings based on Library of Congress holdings through 1974 and hence updates the two previous items.

35

LOCATING PUBLISHED WORKS ABOUT AN AMERICAN
AUTHOR OR WORK

Phase I: Locating existing bibliographies
401 Nilon & Havlice

402 Toomey
403 *Bib Index*

404 *LHUS*
Phase II: Creating bibliographies
A. General bibliographies, American literature
405 Leary
406 MLA
407 *ABELL*   408 *Arts in Am Studies*   409 *TCL*
B. General bibliographical resources
B1. Books
410 *CBI*   411 LC Subj Cat   412 Brit Lib Cat
413 *Engl Cat*   414 Subj Guide *BIP*   415 *BNB*
416 *Essay & Gen Lit Index*   (419 *Biog Index*)
B2. Serials
417 *Poole's* (19th century)
418 *Readers' Guide*   419 *Biog Index*
420 *Hum Index*   421 *Brit Hum Index*
422 *NY Times Index*   423 *Times Index* (London)

403 *Bibliographic Index* (see 304).
A subject index to bibliographies separately published and as
parts of works, from 1937 on. Supplements Nilon, Havlice, and
Toomey by providing more up-to-date listings of both separately published bibliographies and bibliographies that appear
in serials or as parts of books, also of authors not covered in those
works. An essential resource.

404 Spiller, Robert E., Thomas H. Johnson, and Richard M.
Ludwig, et al., eds. *Literary History of the United States:
Bibliography.* 4th ed. 2 vols. New York: Macmillan, 1974, 2.
373–1375. PS88.L522.
The best-known resource for the study of American literature,
this important work is divided into two volumes, the first being
a discursive history of literature in the United States, the second
a collection of bibliographical essays on both subjects and
authors. While the bibliographies of individual authors are not
so thorough as those available in other sources, the subject
bibliographies are extremely important. After late 1972 Spiller

must be supplemented by more recent scholarship. Includes a proper-name index.

PHASE II

Purposes: (1) To provide material for the compilation of a bibliography of any author for whom no bibliographies exist. (2) To supplement and update existing bibliographies of an author.

Level A. Scholarly Bibliographies

The following three items constitute the important serial bibliographies for American literature.

405 Leary, Lewis, ed. *Articles on American Literature, 1900–1950.* Durham, N.C.: Duke UP, 1954; continued in *Articles on American Literature, 1950–1967,* comp. Lewis Leary, with Carolyn Bartholet and Catharine Roth (Durham, N.C.: Duke UP, 1970); and *Articles on American Literature, 1968–1975,* comp. Lewis Leary, with John Auchard (Durham, N.C.: Duke UP, 1979). Continued in "Articles on American Literature Appearing in Current Periodicals," quarterly in *American Literature,* 1929–1990. Z1225.A77; Z1225.L492; Z1225.L49.
These three cumulations plus the quarterly continuations constitute the most complete bibliography of articles on American literature. The cumulations subsume the quarterly bibliographies appearing in *American Literature* and expand them considerably. Must be supplemented for books but supplements the MLA Bibliography by covering non-U.S. scholarship before 1956. No indexes.

406 *MLA International Bibliography* (see 306).
The American literature section of this bibliography constitutes the most thorough annual listing of scholarship in the field, but is limited from 1921 to 1955 to work done in the U.S. only. From 1981 it carries a detailed subject index, with authors

treated as subjects. From 1963 on the MLA Bibliography can be searched by computer.

407   *Annual Bibliography of English Language and Literature* (see 307). Lists scholarship done on many American authors, and while it duplicates in the main the listings of the MLA Bibliography and of the Leary cumulations, it picks up listings not appearing in them. Also lists reviews of books. Index appears in each volume.

408   Cohen, Hennig, ed. *Articles in American Studies, 1954–1968.* 2 vols. Ann Arbor: Pierian P, 1972. Continued annually in *American Quarterly,* 1955–1973. Z1361.C6A7.
A subject index to important scholarly articles on American studies appearing mainly in American and British serials, 1954–1972. Procedure is to consult the Cohen cumulation, particularly its subject index; here authors are treated as subjects. From 1969 to 1972 one must scan the "Literature" section and other relevant sections of the bibliography as it appears in either the summer or August issue of *AQ.* The bibliography ceased publication in 1973. Can also be supplemented by the data base *AHL (American History and Life),* from ABC-Clio (covers 1964–).

409   Pownall, David, ed. *Articles on Twentieth Century Literature* (see 315).
Listings duplicate those of the MLA Bibliography, Leary, and *ABELL,* except for ephemeral items and occasional articles appearing in foreign journals not indexed elsewhere. Chiefly useful because of its informative annotations. Limited to twentieth-century writers.

Level B1. Books

410   *Cumulative Book Index* (see 317).
An important index which treats authors as subjects. Theoretically it extends coverage back to 1898, but coverage is limited from 1898 to 1927. The most complete catalogue available, for American books, of authors as subjects. Extends the coverage of the LC Subject Catalog (322) back from 1945.

411   *Library of Congress Catalogs: Subject Catalog* (see 322).
Limited to books for which Library of Congress cards are issued, 1945–, but still an essential index to books about authors. Provides subject indexing of all books submitted for copyright in the U.S., and hence acts as a general subject index to American books, 1945–, and to books printed before 1945 that have been recatalogued.

412   *The British Library General Catalogue of Printed Books to 1975* (see 316).
As it treats authors as subjects, the British Library Catalogue provides access to many books published in England about American authors. For books published earlier than 1870 (the date at which the Library of Congress began to acquire deposit copies with regularity), the British Library's collection is the most complete in the world. For books published before 1945 (the cutoff date of the LC Subject Catalog) the BL Catalogue provides the most useful retrospective cumulated index of books about American writers. See the discussion of its American counterpart, the *National Union Catalog* (708, 712, and 713) below.

413   *The English Catalogue of Books* (see 320).
Including as it does some books published in the U.S., this item provides partial coverage of nineteenth-century books that are otherwise inaccessible through previously listed indexes. It also lists books about American authors published in the U.K. For British books about American authors printed from 1950 on, see the *BNB* (415) below.

414   *Books in Print* [Subjects] (see 323).
An index by subject of *Books in Print* and the *Publishers' Trade List Annual,* this set provides coverage that complements the *CBI* and the LC Subject Catalog, from 1958 on.

415   *British National Bibliography* (see 318).
An extension of the British Library Catalogue, this subject index provides authoritative and up-to-date listings of British books about American authors, from 1950 on.

416 *Essay and General Literature Index* (see 324).
Since it indexes essays and articles appearing in collections, miscellaneous volumes, and the like, it provides the only analysis of such items. Authors are treated as subjects. From 1947 this function is filled for authors by the *Biography Index* (327, 419).

Level B2. Serials

417 *Poole's Index* (see 325).
Arranged as a subject catalogue of American and British periodicals, 1802–1907, *Poole's* provides material about American authors appearing in both British and American serials during that period. Please note especially Wall's *Cumulative Author Index* (325), which provides more detailed indexing of authors in *Poole's*.

418 *Readers' Guide to Periodical Literature* (see 326).
Provides indexing of American serials from 1900 on, treating authors as subjects. From 1947 on, consult also the *Biography Index* (327). The *Readers' Guide* is crucial to any research on recent and contemporary writers, for locating material about them that might appear in magazines of general circulation.

419 *Biography Index* (see 327).
A thorough treatment of authors as subjects. For this purpose, from 1947 on it supplants both the *Readers' Guide* (418) and the *Essay and General Literature Index* (416).

420 *Humanities Index* (see 329).
Provides indexing by author (as subject) of serials of a scholarly nature, not usually indexed elsewhere. An important source.

421 *British Humanities Index* (see 328).
Indexes British periodicals of a scholarly or intellectual nature, treating authors as subjects and hence provides coverage of

scholarship done in Great Britain on American literary figures. Useful complement to the American sources.

422 *The New York Times Index* (see 331).
The subject index to our national newpaper of record for the twentieth century and an important paper for the nineteenth, this index provides an extraordinary amount of information about American writers.

423 *The Times Index, Palmer's Index to the Times (London)* (see 330).
The two subject indexes to the *Times* of London, providing access to material on American writers who might have had occasion to appear in the news abroad.

Further Biographical Aids

As I mentioned above, biographical research per se depends heavily on a knowledge of complex and ample library resources, and ultimately on exhaustive research into local archives and personal papers. Library aids to such a search are given in Chapter VIII. A sound listing and analysis of library aids to a search for biographical information can be found in Sheehy (1) AJ60–95. I note one useful item below.

424 Johnson, Allen, and Dumas Malone, et al., eds. *Dictionary of American Biography.* 11 vols. New York: Scribner's, 1964; Supplements 1–8 (New York: Scribner's, 1944–1988). E176.D56.
The most authoritative biographical dictionary of American personages who died before 1970. More limited than some newer items, but articles are very full and contain bibliographical citations. For an index of both main set and supplements see *Dictionary of American Biography. Comprehensive Index* (New York: Scribner's, 1990). *Concise Dictionary of American Biography: Complete to 1960,* 3rd ed. (New York: Scribner's, 1980), provides epitomes of the fuller entries, through the 6th supplement. For further information see Walford (2) 2. 5271, and Harner (3) Q3380.

SAMPLE PROBLEMS

1. I am doing research on e. e. cummings and would like to find out what has been published about him.

The exercise calls for the location of material published about cummings, so the first step would be to determine whether any published bibliographies of cummings exist, which we can do first by consulting Nilon and Havlice (401) and Toomey (402) and supplementing them with the *Bibliographic Index* (403). The second step would lead us through as much of Phase II as would be necessary to allow us to accumulate material sufficient to our needs.

2. I need to determine if any bibliographies of F. Scott Fitzgerald have been published in the last three years.

The topic calls for us to locate bibliographies of, not works about, so we must turn to Phase I of our search system. The best and most recent information can be found in the *Bibliographic Index* (403), which is the most up-to-date listing of both separately published bibliographies and of bibliographies that are parts of other works.

3. I found a scholarly article, published in 1980, cited only by author and title in a book on W. S. Merwin, but I can't find any mention of it in the MLA Bibliography. Where else can I look?

The most likely place to look is *ABELL* (407), which often lists articles not listed in MLA. One might also consult the quarterly bibliography in *American Literature* (405). Leary (405) cannot be used here because it is not recent enough in its coverage.

4. Sam Shepard was profiled in an article appearing in an English magazine in 1978, and I would like to find more information about it.

The most likely indexes to provide information about material appearing in an English magazine would be the *British Humanities*

Index (421) and the *Humanities Index* (420). Another possibility might be either MLA Bibliography (406) or *ABELL* (407), but these would be remote possibilities, unless the profile appeared in a scholarly journal.

5. I have found a citation in the *Readers' Guide* of an article about Tom Robbins, an American author, which appeared in *Holiday* magazine. Now I would like to locate a copy of the particular issue of the magazine in a nearby library. Where might I find such information?

Holdings of journals and magazines or, in library jargon, of serials can be found in *ULS* (628) and *New Serial Titles* (629) in Chapter VI. It is frequently the case, however, that libraries carry computer-accessible union lists of serials for the region in which they are located. In that case you should check these lists first.

6. What bibliographies of Ernest Hemingway were published before 1969?

You should consult Nilon (401) and supplement that information with Havlice for periodicals that may not be covered by Nilon.

7. I need to locate an article about Nathaniel Hawthorne that appeared in a popular American magazine, published in 1837. How can I locate it?

This calls for the location of an article in a nineteenth-century American periodical, so *Poole's Index* (417) would be the most likely route.

8. In 1951 Dashiell Hammett was involved in some controversy having to do with the Communist party in the U.S. Where can I find a contemporaneous account of the episode?

This calls for the location of information about an event having to do with the U.S. government in the 1950s, so *The New York Times Index*

(422) would likely provide it. One might also consult *The Times Index* (London) (423), perhaps also the *Readers' Guide* (418) for magazine coverage.

9. I have decided to do a paper investigating the conditions in America during the 1920s, the time in which *The Great Gatsby* is set. I have had no experience doing any research in U.S. history. Where might I go to gain a knowledge of library resources in the field?

When we need to gain expertise in a related discipline it is always advisable to consult both (1) Sheehy (1) and Walford (2) before we attempt to comb the card catalogues. In both volumes one may find helpful sections on bibliographies of U.S. history. Of particular help here, though it is not introduced till later in the book, are *Literary History of the United States* (404) and *Harvard Guide to American History* (802).

10. I need a thorough list of magazine articles and anthologized essays on Richard Wilbur, published in the U.S., 1970–1979. Where can I find the most complete list?

Remember that we are trying to find articles about, not by, Wilbur. The quickest source is *Biography Index* (419), which analyzes books, magazines, and anthologies and collections, 1947–. One would find partial information also in the *Readers' Guide* (418) and the *Humanities Index* (420).

11. I heard of a book published in the U.S. in 1982 on Nathaniel Hawthorne. I would like to find its title and purchase a copy. How can I find the information I need?

Such recent information, particularly about the availability of a book on the commercial market, can be found in *Books in Print* [Subjects] (414).

EXERCISES

1. What books about Edith Wharton are still in print in the U.S.? In England?

2. What bibliographies of Herman Melville have been published?

3. Outline a plan for compiling a complete bibliography of criticism of any one of these works: *Moby-Dick, Leaves of Grass, The Great Gatsby, The Country of the Pointed Firs,* Emily Dickinson's poetry.

4. Compile a bibliography of works about any American author for whom no bibliography is listed in items 401–403.

V

LOCATING WORKS ABOUT A SUBJECT

This chapter excludes treatment of authors or works as subjects. For coverage of authors or works, see Chapters III and IV.

Of all the aspects of library searching covered by guides to literary research, the problem of locating material on a given subject is the least understood and also the single area in which our bibliographies and resources in literature are least adequate. Yet, ironically, almost all our libraries are arranged according to two great subject systems: the Dewey decimal system, followed by most public libraries, and the Library of Congress system, preferred by academic libraries.

Because our interest in literature has moved significantly from the biographical to an interest in subjects, we have more need now to understand how we can gain access to materials on a given subject (I include under "subject" the study of literary forms) and how we can better inform ourselves, whether it be on the picaresque tradition or the pastoral romance, on Anglo-Saxon burial rites or the building of the Brooklyn Bridge, on hermeticism in the Renaissance or analytical philosophy in this century.

The purpose of this chapter is to introduce you to the subject indexes now available in most library reference and bibliography departments, to explore their distinctions, and to show how they can be fitted together into some manageable system. As in the earlier chapters, we begin with bibliographies of bibliographies, which provide you with bibliographies that have already been compiled and, depending on their thoroughness and reliability, may save you considerable time; and we then cover the indexes proper, which allow you to update bibliographies already published or to create your own working bibliography.

Much of your success in dealing with subject indexes depends on your being creative and ingenious in thinking up subject listings appropriate to your search. Many students find themselves frustrated by subject searches simply because they do not pursue a large enough or varied enough group of subject headings to allow themselves access to the diverse subject-indexing systems employed by various indexes. For example, imagine your chagrin were you to discover rather late in your search that in the Library of Congress subject system all material about World War I is classified under the heading "European War, 1914–1918." You must be creative, experimental.

Of particular value in this regard is the guide to the subject indexing system used by the Library of Congress:

501   *Library of Congress Subject Headings.* 12th ed. 3 vols. Washington, D.C.: Library of Congress, 1989. Z695.U4749.

     The definitive catalogue of subject headings used in the Library of Congress cataloguing system, it provides ample cross-references to alternative subject headings and allows one to gain access to the Library of Congress system (and hence to any index or library organized by that system). Not only is it an index to the Library of Congress system generally, but it serves as an index to any library's subject card-catalogue file, so long as it uses the Library of Congress system. An essential resource.

Of particular use in traversing the distances between the various major subject-indexing systems is the following:

502   Atkins, Thomas V., and Rona Ostro, eds. *Cross Reference Index: A Guide to Search Terms.* 2nd ed. New York: R. R. Bowker, 1989. Z695.A954.

     Atkins and Ostro provide general cross-references among the best-known subject cataloguing systems: the Library of Congress, the *Readers' Guide to Periodical Literature,* the *New York Times,* and the Sears system, which is used by most public libraries.

The computer data bases that are now being developed will measurably improve our ability to deal with subjects. You need to think particularly of the possibilities afforded by computer searching of such data bases as *AHL* (408), MLA (306), *CBI* (410), the various Wilsonline data bases like *BIO* (327) and *HUM* (329), and the *Magazine Index* data base (326). Since computer searching requires extensive skills, I recommend you read Rosa Oppenheim, "Computerized Bibliographic Searching in Literary Study," and Therese Villella, "Four Humanities Databases on DIALOG: Contents and Search Strategies," *Literary Research Newsletter* 10 (1985): 17–50. I also recommend you develop a working relationship with a good reference librarian who knows the ins and outs of searching computer data bases. Harner (3), section 1, provides excellent guidance also.

Review the flowchart before continuing.

LOCATING WORKS ABOUT A SUBJECT

Phase I: Locating existing bibliographies
A. General bibliographies of bibliographies
503 Besterman & Toomey
504 *Bib Index*
B. Bibliographies of bibliographies in literature
505 Howard-Hill (British)
506 Nilon (American)

Phase II: Creating bibliographies
A. Literature
A1. English literature, general bibliographies
507 *NCBEL*   508 MLA
509 *ABELL*
A1a. Period bibliographies 510–514
A2. American literature, general bibliographies
515 *LHUS*   516 Leary   517 *Arts in Am Studies*
518 MLA Bibliography
B. General resources
B1. Books (chronologically)
520 Fo Lib Cat (1475–1700)
521 Peddie   522 *Engl Cat*
524 *New Sabin* (19th Century)
523 BL Subj Cat   525 LC Subj Cat   526 *CBI*
527 *BNB*
528 Subj Guide *BIP*
529 *Whitaker's*   530 *Engl Cat*   531 *British BIP*
532 *Essay & Gen Lit Index*
B2. Serials
533 *Poole's* (19th century)
534 *Readers' Guide*   535 *Hum Index*
536 *Brit Hum Index*
537 *NY Times Index*   538 *Times Index* (London)

PHASE I

Purpose: To find what bibliographies on a given subject exist.

Level A. General Bibliographies of Bibliographies

503 Besterman. *A World Bibliography of Bibliographies;* Toomey, *A World Bibliography of Bibliographies, 1964–1974* (see 303).

The most frequently consulted subject bibliography, international in scope, catalogues by subject separately published bibliographies only, from earliest times through 1963. Besterman's subject indexing is very general, tends to rely on proper-name subjects, but does include entries on literary genres broadly treated (drama and stage, fiction, but not epic, pastoral). Toomey continues Besterman, limiting itself to Library of Congress acquisitions from 1964 to 1974, and using generally the *Library of Congress Subject Headings* (501), for its subject indexing system and so provides more detailed indexing than does Besterman.

504 *Bibliographic Index* (see 304).

Provides continuing complementary coverage to Besterman and Toomey from 1937 on by indexing by subject both separately published bibliographies and also bibliographies that are parts of larger works. Scope limited mainly to English- and Continental-language items. Helpful subject indexing, with ample cross-references, especially of literary forms (e.g., epic poetry, pastoral poetry, poetry: women authors, and the like). For searches of bibliograpies of literary forms it is more useful than either Besterman or Toomey because of its more accessible indexing system.

Level B. Bibliographies of Bibliographies in Literature

505 Howard-Hill. *Index to British Literary Bibliography,* 1 (rev. ed., 1987), 3–4, 6 (see 301).

Provides a bibliography of bibliographies of books about various subjects, ranging from fencing to rhetoric to tennis, limited to books published after 1890, through 1969, stressing avocational interests, hobbies, sports. Not exhaustive but provides a useful list of old catalogues of subject collections, personal libraries, and the like.

506 Nilon, *Bibliography of Bibliographies in American Literature* (see 401).

Provides some general subject indexing of bibliographies in American literature, through 1969, under such topics as folklore, humor, regionalism, science, cinema, children's literature. The subject section of Nilon is somewhat disappointing as the materials for an excellent "Besterman" for American literature and culture are close at hand but are really not used to best advantage.

PHASE II

Purposes: (1) To provide materials for the compilation of a bibliography of any subject for which none exists. (2) To supplement and update existing bibliographies.

Level A. Resources in Literature

Level A1. English Literature, General Bibliographies

507 *The New Cambridge Bibliography of English Literature* (see 302); supplemented by *The Cambridge Bibliography of English Literature,* ed. F. W. Bateson, 4 vols. (Cambridge: Cambridge UP, 1941); Supplement, ed. George Watson (Cambridge: Cambridge UP, 1957).

The most complete retrospective bibliographical accumulation of materials on English literature, the *NCBEL* provides excellent subject bibliographies in each volume, covering the period 600–1950, both on literary forms and on cultural matters. Volumes contain bibliographies on subjects like education, travel, politics, book production and distribution, and other primarily intellectual subjects. Coverage of subjects is uneven from volume to volume, and for the eighteenth- and nineteenth-century periods (and to a lesser extent in the other periods) the earlier *CBEL* and its supplement contain excellent subject bibliographies, now somewhat out of date, that were dropped in the preparation of the *NCBEL*.

508   *MLA International Bibliography* (see 306).
Beginning with the 1981 issue of this annual bibliography, it contains two alphabets: a listing of scholarship by author and general subject, arranged by literature (American, English, Spanish, etc.), followed by a listing by subject, which is cross-referenced to the first listing. This new subject index, long overdue, is a marvel to use. In addition, previous issues of the MLA Bibliography, back through 1963, are accessible through a computerized keyword subject searching process, which eventually will cover all the MLA bibliographies issued to date. Otherwise the MLA Bibliography before 1968 provides very limited subject access, mostly to major genres and to background studies.

509   *Annual Bibliography of English Language and Literature* (see 307).
Provides very useful subject indexing of a general nature on English literature, with emphasis on philological topics. Most recently it includes a section on the use of computers in the study of literature, on folklore, and various genres (both generally and by literary period). Each volume contains an author-subject index, with limited subject entries.

Level A1a.   English Literature, Period Bibliographies

510   Greenfield and Robinson, *A Bibliography of Publications on Old English Literature to the End of 1972* (see 308).
Limited subject indexing of scholarship through 1972, primarily of genres, themes, historical background, style, and language.

511   "Literature of the Renaissance" (see 311).
Provides limited subject indexing for both English and Continental literature, stressing mainly bibliographical works, drama and stage, and a general category titled "History, Manners, and Customs." Includes index of proper names.

512 "English Literature, 1660–1800" (see 312).
    Contains especially valuable general subject sections on politi-
    cal and social background; philosophy, science, and religion;
    literary history and criticism; and Continental background.

513 "The Romantic Movement: A Selective and Critical Bibliogra-
    phy" (see 313).
    Very limited subject analysis, in three general sections, on
    bibliographical studies, on environment (art, society, politics,
    and religion), and criticism. The Elkins and Forstner cumulati-
    ons provide only proper-name subject indexing.

514 "Victorian Bibliography" (see 314).
    Provides limited subject coverage under the following general
    subject headings: bibliographical studies, movements of ideas and
    literary forms, and economic, political, religious, and social
    environment.

Level A2. American Literature, General Bibliographies

515 *Literary History of the United States: Bibliography* (see 404).
    Vol. 2, the bibliography, contains important listings for such
    topics as folk literature, Indian lore and antiquities, popular
    literature, sections on regional literature, slavery and conflict.

516 Leary, *Articles on American Literature* (see 405).
    The Leary cumulations provide roughly twenty to twenty-five
    subject heading analyses, which are useful but which cover only
    articles. Some examples: language and style, poetry, philosophy
    and philosophical trends, religion, science, women, humor. The
    quarterly bibliographies appearing in *American Literature* con-
    tain only brief mention of scholarship on various genres, under
    the three historical divisions of that bibliography.

517 *Articles in American Studies* (see 408).
    For the period covered this bibliography provides listings of
    articles only, 1954–1972, in many areas of American culture,
    by subject. Some important listings: art and architecture,
    economics, education, foklore, philosophy, psychiatry and
    psychology. The Cohen cumulation, 1954–1968, contains a

proper-name subject index. This bibliography was discontinued with the 1972 issue. From 1964 on the computer data base *AHL* can be helpful.

518 *MLA International Bibliography* (see 306).
A full account of the general subject indexing of this item is given in item no. 508. In the American literature section, before 1970, the subject indexing is limited to "General and Miscellaneous," with few subdivisions subsumed. From 1963 on subject searching is best achieved by using the computer data base. From 1981 on the MLA Bibliography provides a detailed subject index to the bibliography proper.

Level B. General Resources

Level B1. Subject Indexes to Books

Rather than distinguish between American and British indexes, both are covered simultaneously and in chronological order, proceeding from subject indexes for earliest printed books to the most recent.

519 *Accessing Early English Books, 1641–1700: A Cumulative Index to Units 1–32 of the Microfilm Collection.* 4 vols. Ann Arbor: University Microfilms, 1981–. Z2002.U586.
This is a most helpful title and subject index to the first thirty-two of a total of sixty-one units of the Wing Early English Books series, or approximately 26,000 of a total of 90,000 items, being microfilmed by University Microfilms International (see also 606). When complete it will represent the best available form of subject index for all books published in England and certain other countries from 1641 through 1700. Since the subject indexing is done according to the Library of Congress system, potential subject headings can be found by consulting 501.

520 *Catalog of Printed Books of the Folger Shakespeare Library.* 28 vols. Boston: G. K. Hall, 1970. Supplements 1 and 2 (1976, 1981). Z8813.F6.
Since the Folger Library constitutes the largest single holding in the world of English books of the Renaissance, a catalogue of

that collection is invaluable. In this instance it provides some form of subject indexing that is not provided by the *STC* (see 605 below) and is limited for Wing (see 519 above). A single author-title-subject index, reproducing printed cards for all books in the library, it utilizes for its subject indexing the Library of Congress cataloguing system. Thus the *Subject Headings* index (see 501) can be used to gain access to subject listings of this important collection. Includes all books in the library regardless of date. The most useful subject index to Renaissance books in lieu of a subject index to the *STC* and Wing.

521 Peddie, R. A. *Subject Index of Books Published Before 1880.* 4 vols. London: Grafton, 1933–1948. Z1035.P37, P38.
     A subject index primarily of British books published before 1880, which attempts to extend the coverage of the British Library Subject Index (523 below), limiting itself to a total of about 200,000 volumes and to subjects not ordinarily covered in more general library catalogues. Based mainly on British Library holdings. Each volume constitutes a separate alphabetical subject catalogue, with vol. 3 containing also a cumulative analysis of the subject headings used in the first three volumes. Cumbersome, but useful for locating books by subject from 1475 to 1880. See also 611, especially the *ESTC* computer data base.

522 *The English Catalogue* (see 320).
     Provides subject indexing of a limited nature for English books, 1801–1967. The years 1801–1837 are covered in a retrospective volume edited by Peddie and Waddington. The subject index is limited to keyword-title entries, i.e., to be listed the subject must appear in the title of the item. A restricted but still useful subject index to nineteenth-century British books.

523 *The British Library General Subject Catalogue* [1881–]. London: British Library, 1902–. Z1035.B8613.
     A subject index to books added to the British Library from 1881, which supplements the British Library Catalogue, since that catalogue treats persons as subjects and also contains a few general subject entries. Subject indexing through 1950 is frequently difficult to follow and broad rather than specific; from 1951 on it is much more useful. Since the 1975–1985

cumulation, the catalogue is available on microfiche only. For subject indexing of modern British books from 1950 on, consult first the *BNB*, 527.

524 *The New Sabin* (see 710). Z1201.T45.

A recataloguing and expansion of Sabin's *Bibliotheca Americana*, coordinated with the microform series of Americana issued by the Lost Cause Press of Louisville, Kentucky. Eight volumes to date, in progress. Sabin is an extremely valuable collection of books but difficult to use because of the lack of a subject index. *The New Sabin* attempts to remedy that lack by providing subject indexing to its listings. All volumes are arranged alphabetically by author, according to the order in which items were microfilmed. At present a cumulative author-title-subject index is available for the first five volumes, providing momentarily a limited form of subject indexing for early American books. Indexing is based on the Library of Congress system, but heavily dependent on proper names, and lacking cross-references. Organization and quality of this series is cumbersome and weak, but its subject indexing is still useful since it represents the closest we can come to a subject index for books of this period and topic.

525 *Library of Congress Catalogs: Subject Catalog* (see 322).

A catalogue by subject of books added to the Library of Congress from 1945 on. The most thorough and extensive subject index to books extant, limited only by the time period covered. Uses the Library of Congress subject cataloguing system, which can be cross-referenced in *Library of Congress Subject Headings* (501). Treats persons as subjects. From 1983 on issued in microform as an index of the *National Union Catalog.*

526 *Cumulative Book Index* (see 317).

An index primarily to American books, but including many other English-language books, commencing 1898, but giving full coverage only from 1928 on. Books are listed in one author-title-subject alphabet. Lists ephemeral items sometimes not to be found in the Library of Congress/*National Union Catalog* listings. Highly reliable and extremely useful subject cataloguing and cross-referencing.

527 *British National Bibliography* (see 318).
A subject catalogue of books submitted for "legal deposit" in the British Isles, organized according to the Dewey decimal system, covering 1950–. One of the most thorough and useful subject catalogues, particularly of British books. Its Dewey arrangement makes it a bit cumbersome to use, though the system's organization is provided in outline form at the beginning of each volume. Author–limited title index to the subject catalogue is included. Issued weekly, cumulated every four months and annually.

528 *Books in Print* [Subjects] (see 323).
From 1956 on, a very helpful subject index to American books, limited to titles listed in *Books in Print* and basing its cataloguing on the Library of Congress subject cataloguing system. Provides listings for books that may not appear in the Library of Congress/*National Union Catalog* listings, and, most importantly, provides a list of books on a given subject that are in trade and available for purchase. Issued annually.

529 *Whitaker's Cumulative Book List* (see 319).
Subject entries are limited to keyword-title listings, covering books from 1924 on. Supplements the *BNB,* also continues the broader coverage of *The English Catalogue* from its cessation of publication in 1967.

530 *The English Catalogue* (see 320).
See 522 above.

531 *British Books in Print* (see 321).
Provides a list of British books in trade and available for sale, arranged in one alphabet by author-title–keyword subject. Issued annually since 1874.

532 *Essay and General Literature Index* (see 324).
Provides analysis of collections, miscellaneous volumes, parts of books by author-subject–limited title, using the *Readers' Guide*/ H. W. Wilson system of subject indexing. An essential index for locating material that is incorporated into single-volume collections. Covers 1930–. Issued semiannually and annually.

Level B2. Subject Indexes to Serials

Again, as with Level B1, both British and American indexes are covered simultaneously, first treating *Poole's Index,* which is the only general subject index available for the nineteenth century, then treating twentieth-century indexes in the order of their comprehensiveness.

533 *Poole's Index* (see 325).

The only subject index available for the nineteenth century, covering British and American periodicals from 1802 to 1907, using a system of indexing that is peculiar to *Poole's* but relatively easy to follow, employing both subject headings and keyword-title headings. Genre listings for poetry, fiction, drama, and other forms when the name of the form is part of the title of the work.

534 *Readers' Guide to Periodical Literature* (see 326).

The most important index to periodical literature of the twentieth century, providing information on articles in American magazines of general interest. Indexing is by author–limited title–subject, with very full coverage given to subjects. The *Readers' Guide* uses its own subject indexing, which can be correlated to some extent with the Library of Congress system by consulting Atkins (502 above). The *Readers' Guide* includes subject headings covering the major genres, treats persons as subjects, though for that purpose see the *Biography Index* and other items mentioned in Chapters. III and IV. An important complement to the scholarly indexes.

535 *Humanities Index* (see 329).

Provides indexing of scholarly and intellectual periodicals, complementing both scholarly indexes and the *Readers' Guide.* Subject indexing is comparable to that of the *Readers' Guide,* but with headings that are more detailed and more applicable to topics in the humanities. Entries provided for major genres, with extensive entries for various minor literary forms. The most usable of subject indexes for the humanities, with excellent cross-referencing.

536 *British Humanities Index* (see 328).

Counterpart, for British periodicals, of the *Humanities Index,* listing in two indexes, by subject and by author, with ample subject entries, and especially good indexing of literary forms. Preceded by the *Subject Index to Periodicals,* covering 1915–1961.

537 *New York Times Index* (see 331).

A fine subject index to material appearing in the pages of the *New York Times,* 1851–, providing thorough subject analysis of all important events occurring in the United States, including happenings in the arts. Especially valuable from 1913 on. Many literary topics covered: poets, poetry, novelists, awarding of prizes, literary events of note, etc., though the *New York Times* uses its own subject index, which depends heavily on use of proper names. Prior series extends coverage back to 1851, though indexing is inferior to that of the *New York Times Index.*

538 *The Times Index* (see 330).

A subject index to the *Times* of London, less analytical than the *New York Times Index* but valuable for the access it gives to this important paper. Indexing tends to be general, though indexing of literary topics is more thorough than that of the *New York Times Index,* an important virtue of this index.

In addition to these resources, dissertations frequently provide both useful studies of various subjects and, most importantly, bibliographies that are the result of a great deal of research. See Chapter IX for coverage of dissertation guides.

For coverage of subjects in related disciplines, both Sheehy (1) and Walford (2) provide ample listings, especially in the fields of psychology, philosophy, history, law, and the sciences. In effect, you can create your own research guide to other scholarly disciplines through these two reference guides.

SAMPLE PROBLEMS

1. What bibliographies of criticism of epic poetry have been published?

Since the question calls for the location of bibliographies, not of actual critical articles, the search should begin with Besterman-Toomey (503) and follow into the *Bibliographic Index* (504). Howard-Hill (505) and Nilon (506) provide no help with this subject. Finally, one can add considerable breadth to the coverage by consulting 507–509, *NCBEL* (507) MLA Bibliography (508), and ABELL (509).

2. What studies of the epigram have been published since 1950?

Most helpful here is the *Bibliographic Index* (504) to discover first, through Phase I, what bibliographies have already been compiled. Those bibliographies may then be expanded by your consulting the literary indexes in Phase II, specifically under A1, nos. 507–509 (the *NCBEL*, the MLA Bibliography, and *ABELL*). If you wish you can extend your search into the period bibliographies under A1a, nos. 510–514, as they are relevant to your search.

3. Assume you are preparing to teach a course in Native American literature and need to develop a thorough list of books and articles that would be helpful. How would you prepare such a list?

First exhaust the information available through items in Phase I, skipping over Howard-Hill (505), which is irrelevant here. Then under Phase II, A2, check out the subject indexing in items 515–518. It may be necessary in the older indexes to rely on subject headings using the word "Indian" in their titles.

4. You have been studying poems of the sixteenth century that use images drawn from herbs cultivated at that time in England, and wish to know what herbals and other such books from the period are available.

Two approaches might be used here, the former to seek the location of modern books and articles and from them develop a list of sixteenth-century herbals. This would take you through the usual sources in Phase I and then Phase II. But to locate sixteenth-century herbals, you could turn first to 520, the Folger Library Catalog (520) and from it compile a list of titles, and then proceed to the *STC* (605) and then to the accompanying *Early English Books* microfilm collection for copies of the actual books.

5. You have been planning a study of analytical philosophy in general, and Wittgenstein specifically, with the intention of developing a full reading list on this school of thought.

On one level you can pursue your search through the use of the proper name "Wittgenstein, Ludwig," by following the steps in Chapter III, which should produce sufficient material in itself for your needs. This can be done quite easily. With regard to analytical philosophy, you first ought to develop adequate subject headings through the *Library of Congress Subject Headings* guide (501). Then you could pursue your search through Phase I of Chapter V, and if necessary in Phase II through the nonliterary section IIB, particularly for books, *CBI* (526), *BNB* (527), and the LC Subject Catalog (525). In serials I would suggest the *Humanities Index* (535). If necessary you could pursue your search by going back to Sheehy (1) and Walford (2) to acquaint yourself with the special bibliographical tools available to you in the discipline of philosophy. Of course the results of such an intensive search would be more than ample for anyone's needs.

6. You are reading an American novel with a historical setting—say, E. L. Doctorow's *Ragtime*—and you wish to have contemporaneous accounts of some of the historical events referred to.

By far the most helpful item for such a search is the *New York Times Index* (537), which will refer you to specific stories in that newspaper. Also helpful would be the *Readers' Guide* (534) and for international coverage *The Times Index* (London) (538).

EXERCISES

1. Prepare a bibliography of critical writings on courtly love done in the past fifty years.

2. Prepare a plan of research for compiling a bibliography of critical writings on epic theory.

3. Select a topic, concept, issue in some related discipline that touches on a literary question and prepare a bibliography of writings on it. Examples of "related disciplines" might be the law, history, philosophy, folklore, religion.

VI

LOCATING PUBLISHED WORKS BY AN ENGLISH AUTHOR

Compiling a complete bibliography of an author's work is a demanding scholarly task in its own right, and this chapter and the following one can only begin to identify the resources available for such an undertaking. Author checklisting, a more limited kind of compilation, frequently becomes necessary when you find yourself studying an author for whom no bibliographies of writing exist. Such is usually the case with contemporary authors or with authors of an earlier period who are relatively unknown. The purpose of this chapter is to acquaint you with the library resources that will assist you in beginning such a project. The exhaustive accumulation of an author's writing, however, must ultimately involve many hours spent combing library holdings and poring over the pages of periodicals. Ninety percent of the work can be completed by consulting library resources, but the other ten percent requires an enormous commitment of effort. The purpose of this chapter and the succeeding one is to allow you to compile a reasonably complete list of a given author's writings in published form.

The process divides into two phases. Phase I allows you to determine if any bibliographies of an author's writings have been published. Phase II allows you to update published bibliographies or to develop your own.

This discussion is limited to published works. Some assistance in locating unpublished works can be gotten from Chapter VIII, "Locating Manuscripts and Collections." Works written before the advent of printing (i.e., during the Anglo-Saxon and Middle English periods) present special problems. The single most productive resource available at this time is vol. 1 of the *New Cambridge Bibliography of English Literature* (see 302).

Review the flowchart before continuing.

LOCATING PUBLISHED WORKS BY AN ENGLISH AUTHOR

Phase I: Locating existing bibliographies
601 Howard-Hill
602 *NCBEL*
603 Besterman & Toomey
604 *Bib Index*
Phase II: Creating bibliographies
A. Books (arranged chronologically)
600–1475 (Consult 302 *NCBEL*)
1475–1700
605 *STC*   606 Wing *STC*
607 Brit Lib Cat   608 Sta Reg
609 Greg   610 *Term Cats*
1700–1800
611 *18th-cen STC* (in progress)
612 Brit Lib Cat
1800–1900
613 *19th-cen STC* (in progress)
614 Brit Lib Cat   615 *Engl Cat*
1900–
616 Brit Lib Cat   617 *CBI*
618 *BNB*   (619–22)
B. Serials
623 *Poole's*   624 *Well Index* (19th century)
625 *Readers' Guide*   626 *Hum Index*
627 *Brit Hum Index*

PHASE I

Purpose: To determine what, if any, bibliographies of an author have been published.

601 Howard-Hill, T. H. *Index of British Literary Bibliography* (see 301).

Vols. 5 and 7 of this very useful set, still in progress, provide a list, by author, of published bibliographies of works both about and by a British author. Covers bibliographies produced from 1890 to 1979, with coverage of the earlier period projected for Vol. 3. For bibliographies published after 1979 or for authors not covered here, consult the *Bibliographic Index* (604 below). For authors not listed, consult items below.

602 *New Cambridge Bibliography of English Literature* (see 302).
     Covers the range of English writers, 600–1950, by period,
     providing under each author section a list of published bibliog-
     raphies. Cutoff dates for coverage vary with each volume. To use
     effectively for this purpose, first consult Vol. 5, the index, and
     then the particular section of the relevant volume.

603 Besterman, *A World Bibliography of Bibliographies* (see 303);
     Toomey, *A World Bibliography of Bibliographies, 1964–1974.*
     Provides a list of separately published bibliographies by author
     from the beginnings to 1963 and is extended by Toomey from
     1964 to 1974; also supplements Howard-Hill for the period
     1890 backward. For bibliographies that appear as parts of
     books, see the *Bibliographic Index* (304).

604 *Bibliographic Index* (see 304).
     A subject index to bibliographies appearing separately or as
     parts of larger works, this cumulation is limited only by its
     relatively recent beginning date of 1937. Scope limited mainly
     to English-language and Continental-language items. An im-
     portant source that updates all previously mentioned sources.

PHASE II

Purposes: (1) To supplement and update existing bibliographies. (2)
To provide resources for compilation of bibliographies where none
exist.

Level A. Books (Arranged Chronologically)

600–1475

(Consult Vol. 1 of the *New Cambridge Bibliography of English Literature,* 302, 305.)

1475–1700

605 Pollard, A. W., and G. R. Redgrave. *A Short-Title Catalogue of
     Books Printed in England, Scotland, and Ireland, and of English*

Books Printed Abroad, 1475–1640. Katharine F. Pantzer, W. A. Jackson, and F. S. Ferguson, eds. 2nd ed. 3 vols. London: Bibliographical Society, 1976–1991. Z2002.P77; Z2001.A44 (Allison).

A catalogue by author, and for anonymous works by title, of extant works published within the constrictions noted. Does not include books printed abroad in a foreign language. Since it is based on library holdings, it is a highly reliable source of bibliographical information, though its strict adherence to bibliographical information as given in copies of the books sometimes makes it difficult to use. See also A. F. Allison and V. F. Goldsmith, *Titles of English Books (and of Foreign Books Printed in England): An Alphabetical Finding-List by Title of Books Published Under the Author's Name, Pseudonym, or Initials,* 1 (Folkestone, Eng.: Dawson, 1976). Actual copies of most books are available on microfilm through the Early English Books series by University Microfilms.

606 Wing, Donald. *Short-Title Catalogue of Books Printed in England, Scotland, Ireland, Wales, and British America, and of English Books Printed in Other Countries, 1641–1700.* 2nd ed. 3 vols. New York: MLA, 1972–. Index in progress. Z2002.W48.

A catalogue by author, and where anonymous by title, of extant books published during the period 1641–1700, within the limits noted in its title. Wing continues the coverage of *STC* to the close of the seventeenth century, including books printed in British America. Like the newer volume of the *STC,* Wing's cataloguing is less confusing and more reliable than that of the old *STC.* A helpful aid to Wing is vol. 2 of Allison and Goldsmith's *Titles of English Books* (Folkestone, Eng.: Dawson, 1977; see 605 above). Copies of books are available on microfilm through the Early English Books series by University Microfilms. See also 519. All items listed in Wing will eventually be accessible through the OCLC computer data base (see 713), as a result of a cooperative project among five libraries and University Microfilms International.

607 British Library. *The British Library General Catalogue of Printed Books* (see 315). Supplements, 1976–1982 (50 vols.); 1982–1985 (26 vols.); 1986–1987 (22 vols.).

Though titles appearing in the British Library Catalogue theoretically will have been incorporated into the *STC*, this item should always be checked, particularly where the *STC* and Wing prove difficult to use. As a catalogue of the largest and most comprehensive holding of British books it is indispensible to any bibliographical project. Since, also, it is based on an examination of actual copies of books, its authority is almost unchallenged. From 1976 on available on microfiche. Somewhat less accessible but exhaustive bibliographic information on British publications is available through UKMARC, a data base of holdings in the British Library, which is part of the OCLC computer data base (see 713).

608 Arber, Edward. *A Transcript of the Registers of the Company of Stationers of London, 1554–1640.* 5 vols. London, 1875–1877; rpt. New York: Peter Smith, 1950. Z2002.L64.

An important contemporaneous list of titles intended to be published during the period 1554–1640 and hence a useful supplement to the *STC,* since it may contain titles of books for which copies have not survived. A difficult source to use, since items are listed chronologically (usually without author's name) and has no author or title index. A brief, helpful explanation of early copyright is given in *The Oxford Companion to English Literature* (101) Appendix I.

609 Greg, W. W. *A Bibliography of the English Printed Drama to the Restoration.* 4 vols. London: Bibliographical Society, 1939–1959. Z2014.D7G78.

A descriptive bibliography of printed plays from the beginning of printing to 1660, listing both separately published plays and plays published as parts of other works. Though most titles in this work now appear in the *STC,* it includes also a list of lost plays and contains other items not mentioned in the *STC.* The new *STC* subsumes Greg's titles of extant published works.

610 Arber, Edward. *The Term Catalogues, 1668–1709 A.D.* 3 vols. London: Arber, 1903. Z2002.A31.

A sometimes helpful list of books published during this period, drawn from booksellers' lists. Like the Stationers' Register it is an indicator of books that may have been published, or books that were published and of which copies have not survived, or books that were intended to be published.

1700–1800

611 *The Eighteenth-Century Short-Title Catalogue.* Robin Alston, ed. Computer data base available from RLIN.

A computer data base that draws information from the holdings of the British Library and other cooperating libraries, containing over 300,000 entries, this bibliography represents the future direction of large bibliographical projects of this kind. Access is through RLIN, from Research Libraries Group at Stanford University, by author, title, and through various subject-searching strategies. Also available on microfiche as *The Eighteenth Century Short Title Catalogue, 1990* (London: British Library, 1990), a list by author and title. Available also on CD-ROM.

612 British Library. *The British Library General Catalogue of Printed Books* (see 316 and 607).

To be used to supplement 611 by providing some coverage of areas not currently covered in the *Eighteenth-Century STC.*

1800–1900

613 *Nineteenth Century Short Title Catalogue* [Series I, Phase I, 1801–1815], 6 vols. Cambridge: Chadwyck-Healey, 1984–86; Series II, Phase I [1816–1870], 55 vols. (1986–). Z2001.N55.

A union catalogue based on the holdings of the British Library and others, which eventually will cover books printed in Great Britain, the colonies, and the U.S., and in English abroad, from 1801 to 1918. It adds some new titles but the vast majority of entries are from the British Library Catalogue (316). It is hoped that the *Nineteenth Century STC* will provide much needed subject indexing for books of this period.

614 British Library. *The British Library General Catalogue of Printed Books* (see 316, 607, and 612).

The British Library Catalogue provides the most complete and reliable listing of books published in Great Britain. For the nineteenth century it can be supplemented by the *English Catalogue,* below.

615 *The English Catalogue of Books* (see 320).

A listing (1801–1965) national in scope of books "in trade," based on the weekly trade publications *Publishers' Circular* (1837–1959), and the monthly *British Books.* As it is based on publishers' information and not on actual copies of books it is less reliable than the British Library Catalogue, though it provides a supplement to it by listing ephemeral titles not submitted for copyright, and especially a list of books that may prove to exist.

1900 to Present

616 British Library. *The British Library General Catalogue of Printed Books* (see 316).

Again the authoritative beginning point for a compilation of a checklist of any British author's published writings. After 1975 its coverage can be extended by the *BNB,* below.

617 *Cumulative Book Index* (see 317).

Provides comprehensive coverage of English-language publications, particularly British and American, from 1898 on, though coverage up to 1928 is scanty. The *CBI* is especially helpful in locating items printed by small presses, private presses, and the like.

618 *British National Bibliography* (see 318).

The *BNB* can be thought of as an annual continuation of the British Library Catalogue. A national bibliography of books deposited at the Library, 1950–, arranged by subject, with an author index. For the earlier period, 1900–1949, consult, in addition to the British Library Catalogue, *The English Catalogue* and *Whitaker's Cumulative Book List,* below.

619 *The English Catalogue of Books* (see 320).

Provides supplemental listings to the British Library Catalogue, 1900–1965, and to the *BNB,* 1950–1967, of ephemera, particularly of books not submitted for copyright.

620   *Whitaker's Cumulative Book List* (see 319).
A trade list of publications of Great Britain, based on the weekly lists of *The Bookseller* (to 1970), now on *Whitaker's Books of the Month and Books to Come*. Provides coverage of books in trade, especially for 1968 on, after the cessation of publication of the *English Catalogue*.

621   *British Books in Print* (see 321).
Largely duplicates listings of the *English Catalogue* and of *Whitaker's*; provides lists of books currently available for purchase.

622   *Essay and General Literature Index* (see 324 and 327).
Provides for indexing of items that appear in anthologies and miscellaneous volumes.

Sometimes it is the case that an English author will have published certain of his or her titles in the U.S. only. For coverage of British authors' American publications, please consult the resources under Chapter VII, Phase II, Level A.

Level B. Serials

623   *Poole's Index* (see 325).
Though *Poole's* is a subject index, the writings of authors can be located by first consulting C. Edward Wall, *Cumulative Author Index for Poole's Index to Periodical Literature, 1802–1906* (Ann Arbor: Pierian P, 1971), and then by consulting *Poole's*. Limited to British and American periodicals, 1802–1907.

624   *The Wellesley Index to Victorian Periodicals, 1824–1900.* Ed. Walter E. Houghton et al. 5 vols. Toronto: U of Toronto P, 1966–1989. AI3.W45.
An index of forty-three selected Victorian periodicals arranged by periodical, with indexes to named contributors and to contributors using initials or pseudonyms. Although more restrictive in scope than *Poole's,* for literary studies it is invaluable since it analyzes those periodicals in which much of the significant intellectual activity of nineteenth-century England

occurred. Procedure is to consult the two indexes at the ends of the volumes to locate publications by a particular author. For locations of copies of serials, see 628–632.

625 *Readers' Guide to Periodical Literature* (see 326).
Since much of the magazine writing of British authors has appeared in American magazines, the *Readers' Guide* provides an index to their writings published in popular serials in the U.S., 1900–. Indexes poetry, fiction, and reviews appearing in the periodicals covered by this index.

626 *Humanities Index; Social Sciences Index* (see 329).
Provides indexing of serials of a scholarly or intellectual nature published in the United States from 1907 on, not indexed in either the *Readers' Guide* or in the scholarly bibliographies. As many British writers have published in these serials, this is an important index. Also indexes poetry, drama, and fiction, and reviews appearing in the periodicals covered by this index.

627 *British Humanities Index* (see 328).
Provides indexing of materials appearing in British serials, including belles lettres. Each annual volume contains a subject index and an author index, the latter of which should be consulted for our purposes here.

For more specialized indexes dealing with specific genres consult the resources listed in Sheehy (1) and the supplement under Section AE, particularly for indexes to little magazines.

Copies of serials and holdings can be located through the following:

628 *Union List of Serials in the United States and Canada.* Ed. Edna Brown Titus. 3rd ed., 5 vols. New York: H. W. Wilson, 1965. Z6945.U45.

629 *New Serial Titles* [1950–]. Washington, D.C.: Library of Congress, 1950–. Z6945.U5.
Continuation of the *ULS,* issued monthly with quarterly, annual, and five-year cumulations.

British periodicals can be located through the following:

630 *British Union-Catalogue of Periodicals.* 4 vols. London: Butter-
worth, 1955–1958. Supplement to 1960 (1962). Z6945.B7.

631 *Serials in the British Library.* London: British Library, 1981–.
Issued quarterly and cumulated annually. Z6945.B874.

632 *Union List of Victorian Serials.* New York: Garland, 1985.
PN5124.P4.
Locates 1,847 titles in about 350 U.S. and Canadian libraries.

633 Nelson, Carolyn, and Matthew Seccombe. *British Newspapers
and Periodicals, 1641–1700.* New York: MLA, 1987.
Z6956.G6.

SAMPLE PROBLEMS

1. I found a reference to Roger Ascham's *Toxophilus,* a sixteenth-
century tract on archery, and in order to answer a question
regarding its text, I need to see a copy of the first edition of it.

The *Short-Title Catalogue* (605) will provide a listing of this well-
known title, and if you are in a library that has the Early English
Books microfilm series, you should be able to locate a copy on
microfilm. From there on it is a simple matter to consult the passage
of the text in question.

2. Matthew Arnold published an essay in *Cornhill Magazine,* which
in a later form became the first chapter of *Culture and Anarchy.* I
would like to see the original essay.

This problem, locating an item in a nineteenth-century periodical,
can be approached either through the *Wellesley Index* (624) or through
Poole's and Wall (623). Since this magazine is in fact indexed by the
Wellesley, it is a simple matter to consult the proper volume of that
index and locate the needed information.

3. I would like to make a brief checklist of all the published poems of Philip Larkin, the contemporary English poet.

The first step is to follow Phase I and discover if any bibliographies of Larkin's work have already been done. Failing to locate the existence of any, you can then proceed to Phase II, first to the items dealing with books, particularly the British Library Catalogue (616), *CBI* (617), and the *BNB* (618), and perhaps to items 625–627, and then to the various magazine indexes that analyze poetry. In addition, you ought to return to Sheehy (1) and Walford (2) to see what they suggest by way of indexes to poetry for both British and American periodicals.

4. John Fowles wrote an article that appeared in a popular American magazine sometime in 1970. I would like to locate a copy of it.

The most likely place to find information about the article would be the *Readers' Guide* (625) or the *Magazine Index* data base (326). To locate a copy of the magazine in a centrally located library, see 629.

5. Graham Greene contributed an essay on Henry James to a collected volume of essays published in the U.S. in 1962, but I have no further information about it. How might I locate it?

The most likely place to discover more information about the essay will probably be the *Essay and General Literature Index* (622) or the *Biography Index* (327), which analyze "miscellaneous volumes" or anthologies, since we are seeking information about an American publication of a British author.

6. I can't find any bibliographies of books by Matthew Green, the eighteenth-century poet, and so have decided to put my own together. Where might I find the most complete list?

The question calls for the location of books. This might be done through several of the sources listed, but actually the quickest way of doing it would be to consult *The Eighteenth-Century STC* (611) and the BL Catalogue (612), which would provide a list of books by Matthew Green. Because of the age and relative completeness of the BL Catalogue, it often provides the only list of books by minor or neglected authors. Another helpful source would be *NCBEL* (602).

EXERCISES

1. Prepare a plan for doing a complete bibliography of the writngs of an English author for whom no published bibliographies exist.

2. Prepare a bibliography of the uncollected magazine publications of an English author flourishing after World War II.

3. Compile a list of the foreign translations of an English author for whom no previous list has been published.

VII

LOCATING PUBLISHED WORKS BY AN AMERICAN AUTHOR

All that has been said by way of preface to Chapter VI should be repeated here, but since space does not allow such a repetition of material please read the opening section of that chapter before you proceed. Our purpose here is to survey in some logical order the library resources that will assist you in locating lists of the published works of American writers.

Again, the process is divided into two phases. Phase I allows you to determine if any bibliographies of an author have been published. Phase II allows you to update published bibliographies or to develop your own.

For assistance in locating unpublished works, please consult Chapter VIII, "Locating Manuscripts and Collections."

Please consult the flowchart before continuing.

PHASE I

Purpose: To determine what, if any, bibliographies of a given author exist.

701 Nilon, Charles H. *Bibliography of Bibliographies in American Literature;* and Patrice Havlice, *Index to American Author Bibliographies* (see 401).

Both items provide coverage of author bibliographies generally through 1969.

702 Spiller, Robert E., Thomas H. Johnson, and Richard M. Ludwig, et al., eds. *Literary History of the United States: Bibliography,* 2 (see 404).

Provides somewhat dated coverage of author bibliographies.

LOCATING PUBLISHED WORKS BY AN
AMERICAN AUTHOR

Phase I: Locating existing bibliographies
701 Nilon
702 *LHUS*
703 Toomey

704 *Bib Index*
Phase II: Creating bibliographies
A. Books (arranged by period)
1639–1900
705 *ST-Evans*
706 *18th-cen STC* (in progress)

707 Wing *STC*

708 *NUC*
709 *BAL*   710 Sabin
711 *19th-cen STC* (in progress)
1900–present
712–713 *NUC*
714 *BAL*
715 *CBI*   716 *BIP*
717 *Essay & Gen Lit Index*
B. Serials
718 *Poole's Index* (1800–1907)
719 *19th-cen Readers' Guide*
720 *Readers' Guide*   721 *Hum Index*

---

703 Toomey, Alice F. *A World Bibliography of Bibliographies, 1964–1974* (see 303).
Provides supplemental listings through 1974, based on Library of Congress holdings.

704 *Bibliographic Index* (see 304).
Supplements Nilon and Toomey by providing more up-to-date listings of both separately published bibliographies and bibliographies that appear in serials or as parts of books, and of authors not covered in those works.

PHASE II

Purposes: (1) To provide material for a list of the published writings of an author for whom no bibliographies exist. (2) To update and supplement existing bibliographies.

Level A. Books

1639–1900

705 Shipton, Clifford K., and James E. Mooney. *National Index of
     American Imprints Through 1800: The Short-Title Evans.* 2 vols.
     Worcester, Mass.: Barre Publishers, 1969. Indexes Charles
     Evans, *American Bibliography,* 14 vols. (1903–1959; rpt.,
     New York: Peter Smith, 1941–1967); and part of *Supplement
     to Charles Evans' American Bibliography* by Roger P. Bristol
     (Charlottesville, Va.: UP of Virginia, 1970). Z1215.S495
     (Shipton); Z1215.E923 (Evans and Bristol).
     A short-title author-title index to books published in the U.S.
     from the beginning through 1800, which are listed chronologi-
     cally and described in more detail in Charles Evans's monu-
     mental but erratic *American Bibliography.* Shipton and Mooney
     supplement and correct Evans, and parts of Bristol, which also
     supplements and corrects Evans. Bristol's *Supplement* has a
     separately bound author-title index (Charlottesville, Va.: UP of
     Virginia, 1971). These sets taken together constitute the stan-
     dard bibliographical resources for the colonial and federal periods
     of American printing. The early books themselves are being made
     available in microform through the Early American Imprints
     series published by the Readex Microprint Corporation.

706 *The Eighteenth-Century Short-Title Catalogue* (see 611).
     Because of its inclusion of books in American collections, this
     item provides additional coverage for books with American
     imprints.

707 Wing, Donald. *A Short-Title Catalogue . . . 1641–1700* (see
     606).
     Wing provides cataloguing of books printed in the U.S.,
     1641–1700, but largely duplicates the contents of Shipton and
     Mooney, and Evans.

708 *The National Union Catalog: Pre-1956 Imprints.* 754 vols. Lon-
     don: Mansell, 1968–1981. Z881.A1U518.
     A retrospective author–limited title catalogue of all books in
     the Library of Congress and in about nine hundred cooperating

libraries, it reproduces photographically individual main-entry cards. The largest and most comprehensive catalogue of American books, though for early American imprints the catalogue is limited, since the Library of Congress did not begin to acquire books regularly for copyright until 1870. The set consists of vols. 1–685, supplemented by vols. 686–754. For further assistance in understanding this complex set, its "cousins," and its successor, see Sheehy (1) AA126–128.

709 Blanck, Jacob, et al., eds. *Bibliography of American Literature.* 9 vols. New Haven: Yale UP, 1955–1991. Z1225.B55.
A descriptive bibliography of roughly three hundred selected American writers (when complete), from the time of the American Revolution, and including writers who died before the close of 1930, selecting only writers whose output was primarily literary. Listings under each author are limited to books and pamphlets, which are described in great detail, including distinctions of issues and states, printings, and editions of items. Particularly valuable because of its reliability and because of the many minor authors covered.

710 Sabin, Joseph, and Wilberforce Eames. *Bibliotheca Americana: A Dictionary of Books Relating to America, from Its Discovery to the Present Time.* 29 vols. 1868–1936; rpt., Amsterdam: N. Israel, 1961–1962. Indexed in John Edgar Molnar, *Author-Title Index to Joseph Sabin's Dictionary of Books Relating to America,* 3 vols. (Metuchen, N.J.: Scarecrow P, 1974). Lawrence S. Thompson, *The New Sabin* (New York: Whitston Publishing, 1974–), 8 vols. to date. Z1201.S21.
Sabin is an author–limited title catalogue of Americana, not just of books published in the U.S. Since his definition of "Americana" is so broad, his compilation has come to be depended on as a record of American books, supplementing Evans and providing a useful list of books published in the first half of the nineteenth century generally. For a full description of Sabin's chronological limits, see vol. 29, pp. ix–xi. Molnar is an index both to entries in Sabin and to 170,000 other items mentioned in passing in Sabin. A useful method of entry into a sometimes difficult work. *The New Sabin* represents an effort to produce a new bibliography of Americana based on Sabin but

keyed into the microform series of Americana issued by the Lost Cause Press. Its chief value lies in its subject indexing, treated more extensively in 524 above.

711 *Nineteenth Century Short Title Catalogue* (see 613).
Provides additional coverage of American imprints of the nineteenth century.

For further suggestions of other items less authoritative than those already mentioned, consult Sheehy (1) AA554–573.

1900 to Present

712 *The National Union Catalog: Pre-1956 Imprints* (see 708).

713 *The National Union Catalog: A Cumulative Author List* [1956–]. Washington, D.C.: Library of Congress, 1956–. Z881.A1U518.
A continuation of 708, an author–limited title catalogue of books submitted for copyright in the U.S., and as a consequence 708 and 713 together constitute the most complete single record of books published in the U.S., arranged by author or main entry. The former is retrospective, the latter current, being issued monthly, and cumulated quarterly, annually, and quinquennially. As a result, with some consistency one is able through the *National Union Catalog* to compile a complete list of all copyrighted books (including later editions and translations) of any author publishing in the U.S. From 1983 on, cumulations of the *NUC* are issued in microfiche only. Bibliographic information is also available through the OCLC (Online Computer Library Center) data base, which most academic libraries use to acquire cataloguing information.

714 Blanck, Jacob, et al., eds. *Bibliography of American Literature* (see 709)

715 *Cumulative Book Index* (see 317).
The *CBI* provides a supplement to the *NUC* by sometimes picking up ephemera, particularly books issued in small numbers not submitted for copyright.

716 *Books in Print* [Authors]. New York: R. R. Bowker, 1948–.
   Z1215.P97.
   An index by authors to *Publisher's Trade List Annual* [1874–], an
   annual compilation of U.S. and Canadian publishers' catalogues
   bound together, arranged alphabetically by publisher. Though it
   includes many publishers, it is not comprehensive. It should be
   thought of as a list of books intended to be published, even
   though in fact most have been published. Access should be gained
   through the author index to *Books in Print* [1948–] (New York: R.
   R. Bowker, 1948–, and the *Books in Print* [Subject] (323).

717 *Essay and General Literature Index* (see 324).
   Indexes articles appearing in miscellaneous volumes and collections, providing essential indexing of parts of books, particularly essays appearing in collections.

   For books by American authors published in the U.K., see Chapter
IV, Phase II, Level A.

Level B. Serials, etc.

718 *Poole's Index to Periodical Literature* (see 325).
   Although a subject index, *Poole's* provides the most thorough
   analysis of nineteenth-century British and American serials. To
   locate articles by author, remember to consult first Wall,
   Cumulative Author Index for Poole's Index. Poetry and fiction are
   entered in *Poole's* under the first word in the title (excluding
   articles), and so are difficult to locate by author.

719 *Nineteenth Century Readers' Guide to Periodical Literature,* 1890–
   1899. 2 vols. New York: Wilson, 1944. AI3.R496.
   An index by author-subject to publications in fifty-one periodicals from 1890 to 1899, indexing over 13,000 poems under the
   heading "Poems." Also identifies many anonymous pieces. A
   useful supplement to *Poole's* (325, 718) for literary materials.

720 *Readers' Guide to Periodical Literature* (see 326).
   The most exhaustive index for modern periodicals, indexing
   about 160 serials, listing under author, subject, and, if necessary, title. Should be supplemented by the *Humanities Index.*

721 *Humanities Index* (see 329).
Provides indexing of serials of a more specialized nature,
particularly of journals like the *Kenyon Review, Partisan Review,*
etc. See also its counterpart, the *Social Sciences Index.* Complements the *Readers' Guide.*

For assistance in locating articles by American authors in British
serials, see Chapter VI, Phase II, Level B. In addition, in recent years
several new indexes to little magazines and to specialized magazines
have been developed. These are described in Sheehy (1) AE.

You can locate copies of serials, collections, and the like by
consulting the *Union List of Serials in the United States and Canada* and
its continuation, *New Serial Titles* (628 and 629).

SAMPLE PROBLEMS

1. I found a reference to an eighteenth-century religious tract by
   Jonathan Edwards, titled *God Glorified,* and in order to answer a
   question regarding its text, I need to see a copy of the first edition
   of it.

ST-Evans (705) and its fuller predecessor, Evans's *American Bibliography,* will provide a listing of this title, and if you are in a library that
has the Early American Imprints series and if that title has been
microfilmed, you should be able to locate a copy in microform. From
there on it is a simple matter to consult the passage of the text in
question. Should neither of these be helpful, you can also consult
Sabin (710), which is of course a bibliography of Americana, not of
books published in America, and *Eighteenth-Century STC* (706).

2. Bronson Alcott published an essay in 1867, which I believe has
   never been printed in book form. I need to locate the essay in the
   magazine in which it appeared.

This problem, locating an item in a nineteenth-century periodical,
can be approached through *Poole's* (718) and Wall (325), with some
difficulty I grant, but it can be done.

3. I would like to make a brief checklist of all the published poems of Wendell Berry, the contemporary American poet.

The first step is to follow Phase I and discover if any bibliographies of Berry's work have already been done. Failing to establish the existence of any, you can then proceed to Phase II, first to the items dealing with books, particularly the *National Union Catalog* (712–713), *CBI* (715), and then to the various magazine indexes that analyze poetry, particularly the *Humanities Index.* In addition, you ought to return to Sheehy (1) and Walford (2) to see what they suggest by way of indexes to poetry for both British and American periodicals.

4. John Updike wrote an article that appeared in a popular American magazine sometime in 1976. I would like to locate a copy of it.

The most likely place to find information about the article would be the *Readers' Guide* (720). To locate a copy of the magazine in a centrally located library, see 628 or 629.

5. James T. Farrell contributed an essay on writing to a collected volume of essays published in the U.S. in 1946, but I have no further information about it. How might I locate it?

The most likely place to discover more information about the essay will probably be the *Essay and General Literature Index* (717), which analyzes "miscellaneous volumes" or anthologies.

6. I am trying to locate information about various editions and printings of Sarah Orne Jewett's *Country of the Pointed Firs.* What source would provide the most complete information?

Ordinarily one would first try to locate what is the most thorough descriptive bibliography of that author and consult it. In cases where none exists for American authors before 1930, however, the information will most likely be found in the *BAL* (709). In this case the *BAL* contains a very thorough listing of editions and printings of the title in question.

7. Mary Gordon published a new novel in 1981. I would like to purchase a copy. Where might I look to find additional information about it?

BIP (716) would provide information, in the volume for that year, but it may most conveniently be used by consulting first the author index to *Books in Print.*

EXERCISES

1. Prepare a plan for doing a complete bibliography of the writings of an American author for whom no published bibliographies exist.

2. Prepare a bibliography of the uncollected magazine publications of an American author flourishing after World War II.

3. Compile a list of the foreign translations of an American author for whom no previous list has been published.

VIII

LOCATING MANUSCRIPTS AND COLLECTIONS

In many research tasks you reach a point where published sources are not able to provide the information you need, and you find it necessary to turn to unpublished materials. Too often, however, students who are not well versed in locating published sources turn prematurely to manuscripts, only to be informed that a particular document is available in published form. So before you begin searching libraries for unpublished material, be sure you have exhausted the published sources at hand.

Of particular value in learning the ropes, so to speak, is the following booklet:

801 Thorpe, James. *The Use of Manuscripts in Literary Research.* 2nd ed. New York: MLA, 1979. Z692.M28T47.
Thorpe offers both an overview of library resources that provide guidance in locating important collections and a summary of the federal copyright statute, which now extends its coverage to unpublished materials.

Other helpful sources:

802 Freidel, Frank, ed. *Harvard Guide to American History.* 2nd ed. Cambridge: Belknap P, 1974. Vol. 1, chap. 2. Z1236.F77.
Although this guide is intended for students of American history, it offers much helpful advice to anyone working with manuscripts.

803 Strong, William S. *The Copyright Handbook: A Practical Guide.* 4th ed. New York: Bowker, 1993. KF2994.S75.

A helpful, up-to-date introduction for the layperson to the revised copyright law of 1976. Answers questions having to do with the use of unpublished material and with the doctrine of "fair use" as it has been interpreted both in statute and in case law.

Also helpful in a general way in surveying the holdings of the important libraries in the U.S. and England is chapter 6 of Altick and Fenstermaker's *Art of Literary Research* (8) and Harner (3) section E.

More and more collections continue to be catalogued, but the fact is that most are poorly catalogued or not catalogued at all, particularly those in private hands. In addition to published information about collections, scholars depend on news notes in scholarly journals and on word of mouth to keep them informed of the acquisition by institutions of important collections or of the movement of collections from private hands to institutions.

PHASE I

Purpose: To locate published library catalogues that describe holdings.

804 Downs, Robert B. *American Library Resources: A Bibliographical Guide.* Chicago: American Library Association, 1951; Supplement 1950–1961 (Chicago: American Library Association, 1962); Supplement 1961–1970 (Chicago: American Library Association, 1972); Supplement 1971–1980 (Chicago: American Library Association, 1981). Z1002.D6.
A bibliography of printed library catalogues, union lists of serials, descriptions of special collections, and the like, of library holdings in the U.S., arranged by subject according to the Dewey decimal system, coverage through 1980. Author-title–proper name indexes provided in the main volume and supplements. Though Downs is limited to published catalogues, what it lacks in comprehensiveness it makes up for in usefulness and accuracy, since it not only indicates holdings but also directs you to published descriptions of those holdings. Functions not only as a locater of holdings but also as a bibliography of catalogues of holdings, especially of manuscript holdings. Treats authors as subjects.

805 Downs, Robert B., and Elizabeth C. Downs. *British and Irish Library Resources.* Rev. ed. New York: H. W. Wilson, 1981. Z1002.D63.

The British and Irish counterpart to *American Library Resources,* providing a bibliography of printed catalogues, descriptions of collections, etc., for libraries in the British Isles. Valuable especially for its coverage of published catalogues of the major British and Irish libraries, especially of college libraries at Oxford and Cambridge, and of important catalogues of manuscripts in the British Library.

PHASE II

Purpose: To locate descriptions of collections or of particular manuscripts.

Descriptions of Collections

806 Ash, Lee, et al. *Subject Collections.* 6th ed. New York: R. R. Bowker, 1985. Z731.A78.

A guide to library collections based on responses to surveys of librarians, arranged by subject (using the Library of Congress system). Using as it does the query-response system, the quality of information is uneven, but Ash does cast a broad net and is useful for that reason. Frequently collections that are only mentioned by title in the most recent edition of Ash are covered fully in earlier editions. Excludes material in the *NUC of Manuscript Collections* (808). Treats authors as subjects.

807 *Directory of Archives and Manuscript Repositories in the United States.* 2nd ed. Phoenix: Oryx P, 1988. CD3020.D49.

A handbook to archival holdings throughout the United States, arranged geographically, with detailed descriptions of the various archives. Generally limited to institutions and public depositories. An important item especially for American culture.

808 *Library of Congress National Union Catalog of Manuscript Collections* [1959–]. Washington, D.C.: Library of Congress, 1962–. Z6620.U5N3.

A catalogue, now issued annually, of descriptions of manuscript collections in cooperating libraries throughout the U.S., the information being based on librarians' reports. Items in the catalogue are arranged in order of reporting; accompanying indexes provide access to the entries. The only serial reporting system available, it provides a method of updating other sources and of locating collections not reported elsewhere.

809 Robbins, J. Albert, et al., eds. *American Literary Manuscripts.* 2nd ed. Athens: U of Georgia P, 1977. Z6620.U5M6.

A checklist, arranged by author, of manuscripts of a literary nature, of 2,750 American writers, providing skeletal information limited to identification of libraries and number of items in their holdings. Useful for rapid location of important collections, but provides no information beyond location and size of holdings. Nevertheless the quickest means of locating important depositories of American authors' papers. To find published descriptions of such holdings, see Downs's *American Library Resources* (804 above).

Locations of Particular Manuscripts

810 Ker, N. R. *Catalogue of Manuscripts Containing Anglo-Saxon.* Oxford: Clarendon P, 1990. Z6605.A56.

The most comprehensive index of manuscripts pre–A.D. 1200, containing Anglo-Saxon writings, regardless of subject matter, including a list of lost manuscripts. Lists both public and private collections geographically, with indexing. See also Harner (3) M1645.

811 Ker, N. R., and A. J. Piper. *Medieval Manuscripts in British Libraries.* 4 vols. Oxford: Clarendon P, 1969–1992. Z6620.G7K4.

A somewhat limited but very useful catalogue of pre-1500 medieval manuscripts housed in libraries other than the major British research libraries. Can be considered a supplement to the extant manuscript catalogues for the British Library and the Bodleian, for example. Should also be supplemented by Ricci and Wilson, (812 below).

812 Ricci, Seymour de, and W. J. Wilson. *Census of Medieval and Renaissance Manuscripts in the United States and Canada.* 3 vols. New York: Wilson, 1935–1940. Supplement, W. H. Bond (New York: Bibliographical Society of America, 1962). Z6620.U5R52.
A catalogue of manuscripts of both public and private collections in the U.S. and Canada, arranged geographically, with excellent indexes in vol. 3. Supplement updates coverage by adding titles and providing additional information on manuscripts in the main volumes, particularly on changes of ownership. Somewhat out of date but still useful. For listings in the Folger Library, see their published catalogue, *Catalog of Manuscripts of the Folger Shakespeare Library,* 3 vols. (Boston: G. K. Hall, 1971), Supplement (1987); and in the Huntington Library, see *Guide to Literary Manuscripts in the Huntington Library* (San Marino, Calif.: Huntington Library, 1979), which lists only materials by authors who died after 1600. A guide to the medieval and renaissance manuscripts in the Huntington Library is in progress. For other individual libraries, see also listings in Downs's *American Library Resources* (804) and *British and Irish Library Resources* (805).

813 Croft, P. J., et al., eds. *Index of English Literary Manuscripts.* 4 vols. London: Mansell, 1980, 1982. In progress. Z6611.L715.
An important catalogue of manuscripts of a literary nature, of English writers, organized by author, within the years 1450–1900. Each author entry lists manuscripts by title, giving brief descriptions and locations. Essential for location of manuscripts of literary works but does not record other archival materials, and cataloguing is limited to a specified list of writers, drawn largely from the *Concise Cambridge Bibliography of English Literature* (see 302). Vol. 5, *Index,* in progress.

814 *Index of Manuscripts in the British Library.* 10 vols. Cambridge: Chadwyck-Healey, 1984. Z6621.B84.

An index by author to all manuscripts in the British Library acquired through 1949. It has the advantage of merging the catalogues of individual collections into one alphabet. For more information on individual manuscripts, one must consult catalogues of the individual collections, which can be located through Downs's *British and Irish Library Resources* (805).

In addition to the guides and surveys noted above and the library catalogues they provide access to, specific manuscripts and holdings, particularly those in private hands, can be traced through auction records, which are published in two important annual reports:

815 *American Book-Prices Current* [1894/1895–]. New York: American Book-Prices Current, 1895–. Z1000.A51.

816 *Book-Auction Records* [1902–]. London: Henry Stevens, 1903–. Z1000.B65.

IX

GUIDES TO DISSERTATIONS

With the continuing heavy output of graduate degrees in literature and language, there is a need to have a uniform system of reporting of dissertations and theses. Unfortunately none exists, though the first item, the *Comprehensive Dissertation Index* (901) comes closest to satisfying that need. Still, for complete coverage, you must turn to some additional sources that are perhaps not so well known as the *CDI*.

Probably the most common use of dissertation indexes is to assist one in finding topics for dissertation proposals. A student beginning work on a dissertation frequently needs to find out what issues, areas, works have been covered by previous graduate students. In addition, dissertations are valuable sources of information.

Often they give excellent coverage of topics that are not likely to be covered in published works and also provide valuable treatment of out-of-the-way writers or subjects.

More importantly, they provide extensive bibliographical information about their subjects. Almost every dissertation has appended to its text a bibliography often running to several pages and many titles. These bibliographies are not indexed by the usual sources—i.e., by Besterman, Toomey, Howard-Hill, Nilon, or the *Bibliographic Index*.

Most dissertations from American universities are available on microfilm from University Microfilms International, a division of the Xerox Corporation of Ann Arbor, Michigan. Information about ordering dissertations is given in the entry on the *CDI* (901).

Guides to master's theses are less comprehensive, but some are available. For assistance see Sheehy (1) AH20-22.

901 *Comprehensive Dissertation Index, 1861–1972.* 37 vols. Ann Arbor: Xerox University Microfilms, 1973. Supplements issued annually. Z5055.U49C59.

A subject index (by keyword title) to all dissertations accepted by American universities and some foreign universities, 1861–, divided by general field (chemistry, physics, math, social sciences, language and literature, etc.). Includes also an author index to the main set and to annual supplements. Where applicable, each entry includes a citation to *Dissertation Abstracts,* below, where an abstract of a particular dissertation can be found. The most comprehensive index for American dissertations, though other sources must be consulted to locate foreign dissertations. Keyword subject indexing analyzes only titles of dissertations, not contents, and therefore is not always thorough or accurate. Available through computer data base from University Microfilms International.

902 *Dissertation Abstracts International* [1938–]. Ann Arbor: University Microfilms, 1938–. Z5055.U5A53.

Originally *Microfilm Abstracts,* then *Dissertation Abstracts.* A catalogue of abstracts of dissertations arranged by field, from cooperating universities in the U.S., usually including most but not all universities offering doctoral degrees, from 1938 on. Now issued monthly, with an annual cumulated author-subject index. From July 1969 is expanded to include foreign dissertations. Though not comprehensive, it now includes dissertations from a number of European universities. Indexed by the *CDI,* above, which provides more comprehensive indexing to this set. Valuable in that it allows you access to the abstract of a dissertation, which may contain useful information or may help you decide whether to secure a copy of a particular dissertation. All dissertations listed are available on microfilm or in hard copy from University Microfilms International. Ordering instructions are included in the front matter to each issue. Available through computer data base.

903 McNamee, Lawrence F. *Dissertations in English and American Literature: Theses Accepted by American, British, and German Universities, 1861–1964.* New York: R. R. Bowker, 1968; continued in two supplements, 1964–1973 (New York: R. R. Bowker, 1969, 1974). Z5053.M32.

A comprehensive listing, in the main volume, for American, British, and German universities, of dissertations in English

and American literature, arranged by literary period, individually by authors, and including an alphabetical list of
authors of dissertations. Although the scope is much narrower
than the *CDI*, it provides more ready access to dissertations in
English and American literature and supplements the *CDI* by
including foreign dissertations. The supplements expand coverage of foreign dissertations to some Commomwealth countries
and France. Indexing is by keyword title and can be confusing
and erratic. From 1974 one, one must consult the *CDI*.

904 Woodress, James. *Dissertations in American Literature, 1891–
    1966.* Rev. Marian Koritz. Durham, N.C.: Duke UP, 1968.
    Z1225.W8.
    A listing of dissertations on American literature, arranged by
    subject, treating authors as subjects, in the U.S., Great Britain,
    France, Germany, and elsewhere. Complements coverage of the
    CDI by expanding it to include foreign dissertations. For
    updates, see the quarterly bibliographies in *American Literature*
    (405), which include titles of dissertations completed and
    dissertations in progress. A valuable though somewhat outdated
    complement to the *CDI*.

905 Altick, Richard D., and William R. Matthews. *Guide to Doctoral
    Dissertations in Victorian Literature, 1886–1958.* Urbana: U of
    Illinois P, 1960. Z2013.A4.
    Now somewhat out of date, this guide supplements the *CDI*
    and McNamee by extending coverage to include dissertations
    on Victorian literature not only in the U.S., Great Britain, and
    Germany, but also in Switzerland, Austria, and France. Items
    catalogued by general subject and by authors. Index to authors
    of dissertations.

INDEX

The following entries include both proper names and titles referred to in the text. Numbers refer to items, not to pages. Initial numbers represent the main entry for an item; numbers in parentheses, subsequent references.

ABOUT THE AUTHOR

R. H. MILLER (B.A., M.A., Bowling Green State University; Ph.D., Ohio State University) is Professor of English, University of Louisville, Kentucky. He is the author of many articles in bibliography and textual criticism, on research methods, modern fiction and poetry, and Renaissance literature. His important work in bibliography and research methods appears in *Studies in Bibliography, Papers of the Bibliographical Society of America, English Literary Renaissance, Literary Research,* and *Analytical and Enumerative Bibliography.* He has also published three books in addition to this *Handbook:* an edition of Sir John Harington's *Supplie or Edition to the Catalogue of Bishops* (Studia Humanitatis, 1979), *Graham Greene: A Descriptive Catalog* (UP of Kentucky, 1979), and *Understanding Graham Greene* (U of South Carolina P, 1990). He continues to teach his innovative course in research methods in the graduate English and humanities programs at the University of Louisville and serves as consultant to rare book libraries and academic presses.